# KINGDOM ARMOR
## The Believer's Identity

# Rabbi Yisrael Ben Avraham

Copyright © 2008 by Rabbi Yisrael Ben Avraham

*KINGDOM ARMOR*
*The Believer's Identity*
by Rabbi Yisrael Ben Avraham
HaMishkan
13492 Research Blvd
Suite 120 PMB 435
Austin, TX 78750

Printed in the United States of America

ISBN 978-1-60647-691-8

www.xulonpress.com

Hakkadosh Barukh Hu
The Holy One, Blessed Be He

# Dedication

To my dearest friend Sarah, your prayers, quiet support, kindness, gentleness, patience and meekness. . .shall I go on? Beautiful, simply beautiful, is who you are.

# Acknowledgments

"Eema," Mommie Paula, you are a tree planted by rivers of living water, whose leaves never wither. I bless the Lord for His faithfulness in you. Thank you for your friendship and wisdom.

Apostle Ardell "Danny" and Kim Daniels, I thank Adonai for people like you. I love you both truly and pray the greatest blessings upon you and the Spoken Word family, todah raba; thank you very much.

Apostle Jemal Farrell, my covenant brother; forward we move possessing all we were meant to be in Him who created all things, thanks bro.

To the readers and editor, sincere thanks for your insightful input, editorial skill and kindness you brought to this book. Working with you was a delight.

Yevarechecha Adonay veyishmerecha.
Ya'er Adonay panav eleycha vichuneka.
Yisa Adonay panav eleycha veyasem lecha shalom.

'May God bless you and keep watch over you
'May God make His presence enlighten you
and grant you grace.
'May God direct His providence toward you
nd grant you peace'

BeMidbar (Numbers) 6:24-26

Truly an amazing read!! *Kingdom Armor* reveals "words" to holding life and life-giving substance. Who knew understanding original function and purpose could open doors to true understanding and completeness? This book clearly reveals that God created man on purpose, for a specific purpose and intention.

Joshua Rayburn, Chicago, IL

The bride of Christ must awaken to her true identity and authority in Yeshua. As you read this book get ready to experience a deeper dimension of your kingdom identity in the divine living armor of Yeshua himself. Rabbi Yisrael ben Avraham brings a wealth of insights through Hebraic eyes that give a fresh and broad perspective. You will encounter a transformation in your walk with the Lord, and it will leave you wanting more. This is a powerful and meaty book, and every page is filled with revelatory truths. I highly recommend this book as a valuable jewel to the body of Christ.

Lisa Depew, Dallas, TX

*Kingdom Armor* will shake up and tear down some of the old paradigms of Roman Greco Christianity while establishing a new paradigm based on Judeo Christianity which is our true foundation. You will learn new definitions, new insights, new understandings and new knowledge of biblical passages as you develop your new identity in Yeshua. *Kingdom Armor* is "meaty," which means it is full of "rhema" and revelations. It is not a fast-food meal but a banquet you must feast on slowly as you taste and savor all God has prepared for you. I encourage you to read this book to truly discover who you are in Christ and who God intended you to be in the kingdom of God. Shalom!

Lillie Ferrell,
Associate Pastor of Clear Lake UMC, Houston, TX

# Table of Contents

# Foreword

So shall my word be that goeth forth out of my mouth:
it shall not return unto me void, but it shall accomplish that which I please, and it shall prosper in the
thing whereto I sent it (Isaiah 55:11 KJV).

Through the matrix (womb) the Aleph Bet births the holy
DNA of image and likeness. When we are born again
we are repositioned in our spirit to arrive within the sancti-
fied destination of worship in spirit and truth.

But the hour cometh, and now is, when the true
worshippers shall worship the Father in spirit and in
truth: for the Father seeketh such to worship him. God
is a Spirit: and they that worship him must worship
him in spirit and in truth (John 4:23-24 KJV).

This book presents the pure language of kingdom armor.
It gives explicit directions and definitions. If you will allow
it, a foundation will manifest that should never end.

Call unto me, and I will answer thee, and shew thee
great and mighty things, which thou knowest not
(Jeremiah 33:3 KJV).

Shalom
"Eema" Paula

# Preface

Dear Reader,

Mankind is the image and likeness of Him who made all things. We are the greatest work of God's will in the world. Salvation is the greatest evidence of this work because we are to dwell in God always. God's original intention transcends every comprehensible vantage we may have of ourselves. We are more than what we see, believe or attempt to know. Our identity is more than behavior, emotion or personality. We truly are fearfully and wonderfully made.

Kingdom identity understands the redemptive and restorative process to the living armor of the Lord. I pray that you discover and embrace the divine dimension of your identity that represents Malkhut Hashamayim, "the kingdom of heaven." I encourage you to return to the union in Yeshua with the Father. It is not how much you may know about the Bible or how many times you may have gone through it— but how much instead God's Word knows you and has gone through you. As children of El Elyon, the Most High God, we are light and salt, the distinct radiance and substance of unconditional love. Take what you need.

Rabbi Yisrael ben Avraham

# Introduction

My name is Yisrael ben Avraham. Translated, my name is Israel, son of Abraham. Though I have travelled extensively and lived throughout the world, my home is Jerusalem, Israel. I am a Hebrew who still honors the Torah way of life, and, like Rav Shaul (the apostle Paul), I believe in Mashiach, Yeshua. I have studied at the traditional Yeshiva in Jerusalem and trained under the watchful eye of a caring man as I am perfecting my vocation as a scribe. I am a rabbi through *semikhah* (the leaning of hands, or ordination). Nothing is remarkable about these accomplishments, but I have had to overcome extraordinary circumstances in my life before achieving them.

I have struggled with identity for most of my life, being someone to everyone while being no one to myself. I have wasted valuable time and money and burned a few bridges, and I have many regrets. My life, for the most part, has been a process of privilege and privation; love and lust; dream and delusion. All of this matters not today; in hindsight none of it helped in my understanding of my true identity. They were events and consequences that at one point in my life I used to blame or justify why I was where I was and who I was.

My life began with rejection; therefore I rejected my life. For reasons that are not important I found myself alone in life with no one to tell me how valuable I was and that I occupied a place in this world only I could fill. As a child until my preteen years I was physically abused; this resulted in years in foster care and periods where I was away from my family. I never truly knew my biological father and lived with my mother and stepfather, who was what I call a high holy day Jew. Under very strict rules I lived often with long days and nights of corporal punishment; I was whipped repeatedly with various implements of pain, locked in dark closets for long periods without food and endured verbal humiliation.

I was around twelve years old when I was taken from my parents' house by child protective services. At the time of my initial intake I weighed in at fifty-five pounds at the medical facility where children were examined prior to being placed in temporary custody of protective care. I can remember the faces of the doctors and nurses looking at me with such horror as they traced their hands across my emaciated body. I thought I was normal looking and didn't understand what the fuss was all about, but looking back at it now I must have been a sad sight.

The sad sight was not unusual for the medical professionals who were accustomed to seeing cases such as mine, but my circumstances were a rarity. They were not the result of alcoholism, drug abuse or being a "latch key" kid, for I was from a well-to-do household. My stepfather was a dental surgeon, a Fulbright scholar and a community leader. He was somewhat wealthy with several Bentleys and a very nice house in what would be called an "old money" neighborhood. It was an affluent Jewish community, and we were members of the Jewish Community Center as well as attended one of the larger well-known synagogues. Mine was not the typical child abuse case. On the outside our family appeared to be the envy of many, but in reality underneath it all it was an evil of Satan.

The physical abuse in my childhood at times involved extended stays in a dark walk-in closet. I had a big bedroom with two walk-in closets, a twin bed and one four-drawer dresser. The closet doors had no locks, but the fear and intimidation of my stepfather was so great that I lived in a prison of dread and worry. The fear I had as a child caused me to do whatever I could to avoid a beating, and that closet then became my prison. I recall a summer day when I was sent to stay in a walk-in closet alone in a huge house. But on this day I was so hungry from insufficient food that when everyone had gone out I decided to open the closet door and out of sheer desperation went to a windowsill and ate the chipped paint from around the edges. Again when looking back I now have a better understanding of those faces of shock as their eyes looked upon my frail, bruised and scarred body.

My childhood created in me a sense of worthlessness and fear; being told by someone you will never be anything turns a person into everything they are not. I can remember being in my early twenties and feeling ashamed and out of place with the world because there was no support from family or friends. I began making up things just to be accepted. I recall believing that if I could make myself into someone else all the issues concerning my childhood would somehow just go away. The lines of truth were so distorted as to who I was because we kept up appearances within an honorable and wealthy community. I hated my life of living among the rich while being poor of spirit. I detested everything about me, to the point that all I could do was linger in life until hell could claim my wretched body. Suicide seemed to be the only alternative, but my fear of dying cursed me to live. As difficult as it may sound, the history of my life from childhood to young adult was filled with deception—all because I lacked knowledge of who I was.

Identity or the lack thereof became my biggest enemy. I didn't even have a clear understanding of love to begin with. I slowly denied and devalued myself. I hated everything that spoke against what I knew myself to be. I hid myself from people, covering my shame, and often asked God why He had allowed me to endure such treatment as a child. With all the shuffling in my life at the time, I felt that no one wanted me. I'd learned how to adapt in various cultures in my time overseas, but the adaptation was at the expense of not being who I was on the inside.

Satan has tormented me about my identity for years. Even though much of my situation was beyond my control, the devil would always use my past in an attempt to condemn me. He knew the history I had with myself and other people. In a perverted way Satan had me so twisted that I didn't know who I was or where I was going. I had lived so many lies and sought the approval and acceptance of people, but I had lost sight of my own mind and voice. I had lived in the present based on the past. A lot of things, both good and bad, happened over time, until the day my heart was transformed.

The most profound moment in my life was the visitation of Mashiach. I can't say that my experience was like everyone else's encounter of a divine visitation, but the Lord came to me while I was on my knees crying out. It was during a visit to the East Coast. I had capriciously attended a prayer conference in Jacksonville, Florida. I didn't know anything about the church or the people hosting this prayer vigil. How I got there is still unclear; all I can say is I was there. I remember thinking, *If You are real, help me, please. I don't want this anymore.*

I can't even recall what the "this" was at the time, but a very bright figure appeared before me. It was the brightest light I'd ever seen, and yet I was able to look at it. I was not able to see the face—only a figure of a person.

As the Mashiach appeared, I knew inside that it was He. He reached into my chest and pulled out a small, hard, rock-like black ball of disgusting slime that I knew was my heart. He held it, and before my eyes it went from black to a dark magenta to red to bright red and eventually to the brightest ball of white light I had ever been able to look at without being blinded. Afterward His hand placed that light back into my chest, and the most overwhelming sense of love and joy consumed every part of my being. I cried and cried and cried until there was nothing more; then the figure faded, and I was back with the people who were still in deep prayer.

After this wonderful experience I knew someone loved me and wanted me to live. Though my life had not been pleasant, I had begun the journey to becoming who I always was to the One to whom I meant the most. Before my heart transformation I realized I didn't have the heart to live, nor did I have the heart to die. Without knowing who I was from heaven's perspective, I had no perception of heaven. When we encounter God's love we gain an identity that fills every void Satan has tried to create. The key to identity is to become one in relationship with the One who is. It is critical for believers today to truly abide in the branch so the fruit of Yeshua's name is seen in the earth realm.

Identity is the revelation of who we are as image and likeness. It is man's ability to walk with God, free from deception and darkness. Life is experiencing what was always God's intention for mankind. In the beginning was the Word, and this Word was light, which is the light and life of men. Everything possible fights against this revelation; this keeps many people in an identity struggle, separated from God's love. As humans, we are the crown of creation, created to be the highest function of God's will, a people fearfully and wonderfully made.

> And Jesus said to him, "Today salvation has come to this house, because he, too, is a son of Abraham. For the Son of Man has come to seek and to save that which was lost" (Luke 19:9-10).

The Lord asked something that was never answered in Genesis 3:9: "Where are you?" Yeshua did not come seeking the lost; the Lord, being all-knowing, has never lost His creation, nor did He not know where Adam was when He asked this. Yeshua came to seek what was lost in the garden: the love and the relationship between man and God as they walked as one.

I share a small portion of my life in hopes of encouraging others who have had to cope with similar issues. I had always wondered what I did and why my life had turned out the way it had. I am reminded in John 9, of when the disciples asked Yeshua, "Who sinned that this man was born blind, his father or mother?" Yeshua's response is the greatest example of compassion when things are just beyond a person's choice or control. He said no one sinned, but this was done to bring glory to the Father. This is what I hope you, the readers, will remember concerning those things that are beyond your control. It is the things that are not within our understanding that cause us to question who we are because of the "why" we need answered so bad. "Why did this happen to me?" I have embraced the answer as being because my life is to bring glory to the Father, regardless of the means. I am still alive and have so much to live for—my Creator who made me—and this is truly enough for me.

This book, however, is not about my life, but about the identity every person has in Yeshua, as we war not against flesh and blood but against the spiritual realm. Who we are has nothing to do with what we may or may not possess, where we live or what people of substantial influence we may know. Salvation is more than these things, and blessings are greater than earthly accomplishments.

> For God so loved the world He gave His only begotten Son that whoever believes in Him shall not perish, but have eternal life (John 3:16).

Yeshua is the covering that now clothes believers with a holy identity. He has returned us to where we began. The question posed by the Lord to every believer today is, "Can you love the one I love?" In loving the Lord we discover through His eyes that we are eternally loved and this is our identity.

All of mankind was resting in the loins of Adam; therefore God called all humanity in Genesis 3:9. It is in the "Where are you" call that we have been given the answer in Yeshua to bear once again the light to the world in our living identities. This book is written to bring a deeper sense of who we are in Yeshua's being. We are to live, move and have our being in God's existence of salvation.

> For the Lord favors His nation; He adorns the humble with salvation (Psalm 149:4).

*Beginning—Why the Need?*

This book is about the identity of believers in Yeshua, the armor of the Lord and how they are connected to the kingdom of God. Identity is vital to walking with the Lord. Without embracing the fullness of who we are as believers in Yeshua, we miss encountering the existence of God's original plan for His kingdom. This is not to discount those tearful moments of salvation, but we are to experience so much more as the Lord's children. The nature of identity changes once the revelation of Yeshua is made real. Salvation reestablishes our identity and sets us on the course of forgiveness and love.

Identity can be defined as a person's established psychological identification. It entails character traits and qualities. The etymology of identity is rooted in the Latin *identidem*, a contraction of "idem et idem," which means "same and same." It is also oneness and sameness.[1]

We often encounter two problems regarding identity, one being identity crisis, and another being identity theft. Many people have dealt with an identity crisis at some point in life, often during adolescence. An identity crisis is the conflict and confusion about one's social role, nature or direction in life. In an identity crisis a loss of personality occurs. The other problem is identity theft. Identity theft is the illegal use of someone else's personal information for the benefit of another, usually the thief.

Armor is something that sounds totally unrelated to identity; it is the defensive material made to withstand attack. Over the centuries armor has been developed from animal skins, plates of horn, hardened leather, wood or metal to today's sophisticated Kevlar, ballistic fiber and ceramic plates. Though body armor serves to protect the human body, this armor is no match for the attacks on the human soul. Armor is mentioned throughout the Bible; it served Israel's army in many battles. In Ephesians 6, Paul discusses the believer's position in God through salvation using the analogy of armor.

In recent years the Lord showed me a parallel between the natural and the spiritual; the rise of identity theft throughout the global community was a manifestation of identity thievery taking place in the spiritual realm. I personally experienced identity theft. As a result of this invasion of privacy, my creditworthiness—among many other things—became bad. I was marked as a "subprime" high credit-risk consumer because of identity theft. My risk classification relegated me to the bottom of the financial stack so that interest rates were higher and most lending deals were not advantageous for me. Qualifying for most things became difficult, and this would only compound the issue of rejection I started out with in life.

When I looked at the destruction that identity theft involved, the pattern of Satan's attack was clearer. I became sensitive to what was taking place among believers. I began to see what the Lord was showing me. As the kingdom of God was advancing, so was an attack on its identity.

I noticed the increased number of financial self-help books, conferences and debt-reduction counselors showing up at churches, and I thought this was wrong. The organization of the church had consumed more than it had produced. Believers had become borrowers instead of lenders. Families were being torn apart within a community where unity and like-mindedness were previously thriving. The attack on believers was focused not so much on personal possessions, but on the nature and character of Yeshua which should rule them as children in the kingdom of God.

In studying the armor of God in Ephesians, I began to connect the original attack of the enemy and what was established by God to reconcile the fall of man and the loss of the relationship between man and his Creator. Paul's discussion at a deeper level is about what covers us as we relate the armor to our identity. Though Paul's letter is written to the community in Ephesus, it is traditionally believed it was circulated throughout the region.

It is so important we read the Bible within the context of the time so we properly understand it. Paul was concerned with maintaining unity through the community of believers' conduct when he wrote this letter. The general themes of the letter to the Ephesians are how the plan of salvation is made known to the world by redemption, the believer's walk and how families related to each other.

Paul closes the letter by explaining that redemption is rooted in an accomplished work of Yeshua. At the time of his writing believers were under attack, and Paul himself was imprisoned. Paul concludes the letter by using armor to express metaphorically the body of believers' position in salvation, as well as to express the existence of a spiritual enemy. He gives a list of pieces of armor that protect in warfare, knowing his readers would understand a believer's warfare is spiritual and not carnal.

Spiritual discord is directly connected to the original breach between man and his Maker. Though Paul relates this to the struggle of the present day, his words convey a message about the original breach. Adam's fall in the garden was Satan's attempt to usurp God's identity, which still continues upon the identity of the body of Yeshua. Regardless of what a person believes—whether Jewish, Christian, atheist or agnostic—identity is still the ever-present truth that validates who we are as human beings.

Our adversary is still attacking mankind as the image and likeness of God. In the conversation between Satan and Eve in Genesis 3, the question he poses to her was intended to create a void and thereby an interest in establishing another identity, different from the one God intended. Mankind as male and female was already like God in image and likeness, but Satan asked the right question, and enough space was created to form a desire for something other than God's desire. In the beginning we were one with the Father. All that existed was God. Adam identified solely with his Maker and needed nothing to validate who he was. Adam lacked nothing because all that existed was in him, with him and for him in God.

True identity is not what we have or how we live, though it sometimes appears that way. Identity is the One who created us and seals us in our existence. Our living soul is far more valuable than our statement of faith, our accomplishments or any other standard we use to measure who we are. It is not so much who we are but *why* we are that matters to our heavenly Father. He made us for His purpose and plan.

It is best to understand how interwoven identity, armor and the Hebrew language are before continuing. To have dominion requires an insight into identity, an awareness about the armor beyond earthly comprehension, and the ability to adopt the life of a language. Without identity all authority is false and can easily be shaken. There must be an alignment with heaven to walk in authority. This alignment begins with identity and how God sees His kingdom as He intended.

Identity is a sanctuary because God dwells within it. Man was created in the image and likeness of the Creator. All of mankind is united with the Creator regardless of belief structure or doctrine of faith because of our image and likeness. It is within this framework that God and man are one as it was in the beginning in the record of Genesis 1. The conflicts throughout life will challenge the believer on a daily basis in an attempt to shake us loose from God. The position within the kingdom as God's children is seen within the armor of the Lord; and the battle truly is not ours but the Lord's. It's about position not personality. Where we are in the Lord is more important than how we are; the where will take care of the how because again the battle is not ours.

Salvation is man's covering, and this covering is man's distinctiveness from the rest of creation. Second Corinthians 5:17 states, "Therefore if anyone is in Christ he is a new creation; the old things passed away; behold, new things have come." The newness of every believer is in the name Yeshua and the function of His name. This newness comes in returning to the Creator.

A better way of looking at this is in the example of the moon. Every month there is a new moon. A new moon is not made every month, but the moon returns to its original place as to its design when God created it. Every time we see a new moon, it is as if we are able to witness God's intention for the moon. We see the original state. Kingdom identity in the armor is the same way. Every believer in Yeshua is to rest in Him as born again and as returned to the original place of the Creator's intention.

I will say of the Lord, "He is my refuge and my fortress; my God, I will trust Him." For He will deliver you from the ensnaring trap, from devastating pestilence; with His pinions He will cover you, and beneath His wings you will be protected; His shield and armor are His truth (Psalm 91:1-4).

# Chapter One:

# Linguistics

It is best to lay a foundation concerning the original language of the Bible. The original intent is extremely important to God's kingdom. The people of the Bible, particularly the Hebrews, did not communicate as the world does today. Jews consider the Hebrew language to be the holy language. The ancient Jewish sages believed Hebrew to be the spiritual language of the world. Zephaniah 3:9 says, "For then I will turn to the people a pure language, that they may all call upon the name of the Lord, to serve him with one consent" (KJV).

This "pure language" is Hebrew. One of the ways of learning deeper spiritual truths is by looking at the Hebrew language itself. Hebrew is not a language of description by appearance as are most modern languages. There is a vast difference between the Hebrew and Greek. The ancient Hebrews of the Bible viewed the world concretely, whereas Greek thinkers were abstract in their views. Though biblical history is focused mainly on the nation of Israel, New Testament culture was Hellenistic. Greek became the language of the world during the rule of Alexander the Great and remained the prominent language until the sixth century after Yeshua's death.

The Bible that is commonly read today is from a Greek text written during the Roman Empire. This Greek text of the ancient Jewish scriptures is known as the Septuagint. The name Septuagint, meaning "seventy," comes from an ancient Jewish legend that tells how seventy (or seventy-two) scholars translated the whole collection (or at least the Torah) in seventy days. Several versions of the Septuagint have been preserved, some of which are slightly larger than others. It was first translated and compiled around 250 BCE, probably in or near Alexandria, Egypt.

The language of the Old Testament is represented by what took place more literally. Most modern Western languages are opposite to this and are closer to the Greek language in comprehension. The difference is that Hebrew is perceived using the human senses of sight, sound, taste, smell and touch. The ideas and concepts conveyed within Hebraic context are literal in many ways. When one looks at the Greek, the thought and translation process is opposite; it cannot be perceived by human senses. An example of this can be seen in the word *love*. Love in most cases is seen as an emotion, a feeling. In the Hebrew it is the action of providing protection.

Languages other than Hebrew were used during the time of the Bible, such as Aramaic and Latin. The Aramaic language was the language of commerce; Jews often spoke both Hebrew and Aramaic. Aramaic was spoken mainly outside the land of Israel (see John 19:19; Acts 21:39-40, 22:1-2, 26:14). Biblical Aramaic is closely related to Hebrew and written with the same alphabet. Jewish tradition regards Aramaic as the other half of the holy tongue.

The language of the Bible is very different from the language of today. Rich cultural meanings are interwoven throughout the ancient language. Hebrew is about more than speaking to communicate a point. It is a language full of hidden meanings and messages. Reading the Bible can be a deep experience, not for intellectual stimulation, but for encountering an infinite God who desires to reveal Himself to those who remain faithful in seeking Him. All the languages mentioned played very important roles within biblical culture and in the development of the Bible, but for the purposes of this book the focus will be on the original language of Hebrew. Hebrew is a journey that will unfold the mysteries of God and His people.

*The Hebrew Language*

Biblical Hebrew, especially where the name of a person is concerned, carries character and function. Hebrew is a language that represents the actual character or nature of a person, place or thing. Hebrew is living and descriptively functional. The people of the Bible were not concerned with the descriptive appearance of someone or something but with its role or task. In addition, Hebrew is a very melodious language that speaks in pictures.

In Western culture the use of language is very descriptive of the appearance more so than of the actual function. Throughout the Bible there are repeated instances of names given to a place or person based on something that took place. For example, Genesis 22:14 says, "Abraham called the name of that place The Lord Will Provide, as it is said to this day, 'In the mount of the Lord it will be provided.'" This passage shows the function of the Lord providing; therefore, Abraham calls the place YHVH Yireh (Jehovah Jireh), not just a name for God, but a description of what He did. The words used by Abraham in Genesis 22, "It will be provided," literally mean, "Be seen." This is one example of how Hebrew is living and not just descriptive. Something happened and showed the faithfulness of who the Lord is. God provided Abraham with a place for His purpose.

*Deeper Language Leap*

Within the kingdom of God a language is used to express the greater truth of His kingdom. Hebrew is considered the holy tongue and is held in great reverence by the Jewish sages. It was long considered too sacred for use in certain secular contexts. Hebrew is multi-faceted and full of meanings and allusions that have been lost in translation.

Hebrew was and still is the holy language of God in Israel. It came from within Him; therefore it communicates who He is. It is very difficult, if not impossible, for an English-speaking, Greco-Roman society to grasp this. There is no English equivalent to the concept of a language with a spiritual significance. Hebrew should not be viewed as better than other languages but elevated to communicate God's intention. The English language communicates a point, ideas, feelings and other real expressions; yet it does not convey the function of Hebrew or the Hebrew alphabet. Hebrew letters are the atoms and building blocks of the soul. An example that helps explain how the Hebrew language operates is water. The chemical makeup of water is $H_2O$; there are two atoms of hydrogen and one atom of oxygen. Though this is a simple chemical formula, each chemical element carries a powerful component. The two atoms of hydrogen speak, and the one atom of oxygen speaks. Together they form what is known as water. Such is the same for the Hebrew alphabet. When the letters, each with their divine endowment, are in their place, they will bring about the plan of God. They act as encoded DNA, a continuous and endless chain of God's power.

Genesis 17:15-16 illustrates the power of the alphabet: "Then God said to Abraham, 'As for Sarai your wife, you shall not call her name Sarai, but Sarah shall be her name.'" Here Sarai's name is changed to Sarah. During the time of her unfruitfulness her name was Sarai, spelled left to right with the Hebrew letters *shin*, *reish* and *yud*. This form was masculine and meant "my princess," referring to Abram's princess. Being in the masculine form, her character was unable to conceive seed. But when God changed her name to Sarah, spelled left to right *shin, reish, hei,* her name took on a feminine form, thereby creating a womb able to receive and conceive seed. She went from "my princess" to "princess" and became the matriarch of the entire world; from the "superior one," as Sarai, to Sarah, whose delicate feminine character and nature set the tone for bringing forth the promised seed. The last letter in Sarai is *yud,* the tenth letter of the Hebrew alphabet, which symbolizes order, provision and covenant possession, and carries the meaning "creation." The last letter of the name Sarah is *hei,* the fifth letter of the Hebrew alphabet. It is the same letter Abram was given when his name was changed to Abraham. The added letter is a breath letter denoting grace, redemption and life. This will be discussed in more detail later.

*The Hebrew Alphabet*

In the Hebrew alphabet, letters make up words, words make sentences, and the result is a conveyed thought. If the words are living, would it not be the same for the letters? Just as the Hebrew language is important, the Hebrew alphabet is equally important. The letters are not just random characters but can be considered the raw material that originates in the will of God. Every Hebrew letter symbolizes an attribute of the Lord.

Revelation 1:8 says, "I am Alpha and Omega, says the Lord God, who is, and who was and who is to come, the Almighty." This is written from the Greek, not the Hebrew. For the Jewish people the Greek letters *alpha* and *omega* have no spiritual significance because these "letter" words are in Greek. The Greek translation misses the message of Yeshua. Yeshua is the substance of God's Word as the "aleph-bet" [alphabet]. Together they appear as את; notice how two of these letters are used to spell *emet*, the Hebrew word for truth (אמת). When Yeshua makes the statement that He is *aleph* and *tav*, He is authenticating Himself as the living Word. "Aleph and tav" is a common phrase understood in Hebrew to mean completion or something all-encompassing. These letters are the first and last of the Hebrew aleph-bet. When placed together in this format they convey the message that all twenty-two letters are present. It is like saying "from A to Z." Yeshua is the author and finisher of the faithful.

Hebrew letters are considered "utterances" and should be taken figuratively. It is by these utterances that man is able to perceive the manifestations of God. Thoughts are formulated, and perceptions are developed. How we think and feel and what we desire in life are nothing more than words.

Each letter has been endowed with a certain ability to manifest a particular purpose of God. Just as His Word is sacred, so arc the letters that make up the Hebrew language. Everything we know to exist has come out of the sovereign Creator. Nothing that came into being is not manifest from the Lord Himself. Most people would think this is not important because many languages are in the world today. Some would even venture to say, "God speaks in all languages," and, yes, this is true, but it is not absolute truth. The truth within the language of Hebrew is God's concealment; it brings revelation. He is concealed in order to create a desire for more and revealed to create a response of worship.

The letters of the Hebrew alphabet played a critical role in creation. They assist in understanding the timing and seasons of God. The Hebrew language has twenty-two letters, each equivalent to a numerical value. Numbers do not appear as they do in other numerical systems. Within Hebrew, numbers are letters. For example, the number one is the first Hebrew letter, *aleph*; two, *bet*; three, *gimmel*, and so on. Illustration 1 shows all letters with their numerical value.

Throughout this book it is imperative that the reader remember function as I describe it; I cannot stress this enough. Hebrew is a language that describes based on how things work or what they do. Another thing to keep in mind is that this is not a numerology book, but it is written to reveal the hidden things that are within God's Word. Remember: His Word is infinite and does speak beyond the surface at many levels. The individual letters, their numerical value, their names, their placement within the alphabet and their graphic forms are spiritual in design.

Hebrew is read from right to left; therefore, when looking at the chart, start with the letter at the top right, which is *aleph*. There are five final letters known as *sofeets*. These letters are *kaf, mem, nun, pey* and *tzadi*. *Sofeets* are letters that appear at the end of a line within Hebrew scripture. Included below is a chart of the Hebrew alphabet with numerical values:

Illustration 1

| # | Letter | Symbol |
|---|--------|--------|
| 1 | Aleph | א |
| 2 | Bet | ב |
| 3 | Gimmel | ג |
| 4 | Dalet | ד |
| 5 | Hei | ה |
| 6 | Vav | ו |
| 7 | Zayin | ז |
| 8 | Chet | ח |
| 9 | Tet | ט |
| 10 | Yud | י |
| 20 | Kaf | ך, כ |
| 30 | Lamed | ל |
| 40 | Mem | ם, מ |
| 50 | Nun | ן, נ |
| 60 | Samech | ס |
| 70 | Ayin | ע |
| 80 | Pey | ף, פ |
| 90 | Tzadi | ץ, צ |
| 100 | Kof | ק |
| 200 | Resh | ר |
| 300 | Shin | ש |
| 400 | Tav | ת |

Foundations are important for building a strong understanding of God's Word. Understanding of the fundamentals of Hebrew, the language of the Old Testament, is very essential as a foundation. Without language there would be a lack of understanding. Likewise, without words there would be no expression of thought. And without letters words would not exist. Communication is essential for a community because communion is fostered. When true communion is established, what is held in common is identity. Language is what builds a society, and letters could be regarded as the "DNA" and "soul" of each word.

## Biblical Language Structure

*Figures of Speech*

Both the Old and New Testaments are full of idioms, but the meanings of many of them have been lost over time, creating gaps in comprehension and appreciation. Figures of speech are extremely important to the language of the Bible because of the melodious language that speaks in pictures. The Hebrew language of biblical times had varying figures of speech which consisted of idioms, euphemisms, metaphors and personification.

An idiom is an expression that is unique to a language and cannot be understood simply from the meaning of its individual words outside of cultural context. Modern examples of idioms are sayings like "It's raining cats and dogs," "It's time to hit the sack," and "I'm just pulling your leg."

Some examples of biblical Hebrew idioms are "fallen face," meaning a sad demeanor (Genesis 4:6); for the "heart to melt," meaning to lose courage (Deuteronomy 20:8); "loins," meaning descendants (Exodus 1:5); "grace upon grace," meaning blessed time after time (John 1:16); "give God the glory," meaning to promise under oath to tell the truth (John 9:24); and "if your eye is evil" and "if your eye is good," which mean to be either stingy or generous, respectively (Matthew 6:22-23).

**Euphemism:** The first type of figure of speech I will address is euphemism, something Paul often used. Euphemism substitutes an unpleasant expression for a more acceptable, unobjectionable one to avoid being offensive. An example can be seen in 1 Corinthians 11:30: "For this cause many [are] weak and sickly among you, and many sleep." Paul uses "sleep" here as a euphemism for death. In many cultures it is unacceptable to speak openly about death. Examples are "gone to his reward," "kicked the bucket" and "passed away."

**Metaphor:** Metaphors were also common figures of speech in the Bible. A metaphor is a word or phrase that makes an implicit or figurative comparison. Metaphors, more often than not, cannot be translated literally; they lose the author's intended figurative meaning. A metaphor is frequently marked by a word such as "like" or "as," but not in all cases. Biblical examples of metaphor are "I will make you fishers of men" (Mark 4:19) and "I am the bread of life" (John 6:48).

**Metonymy:** Metonymy is figurative language in which a word or phrase is substituted for another with which it is closely associated. An example of this is seen in Acts 15:21: "For Moses from ancient generations has in every city those who preach him, since he is read in the synagogues every Sabbath." The association of Moses and the Sabbath is that he is the author of what is read on the Sabbath, not that he is the Sabbath.

**Synecdoche:** Synecdoche is figurative language in which a part of something is substituted for the whole, or vice versa. In Luke 3:6 "all flesh" is translated as "all people," "all mankind" and "everyone" and not literally as the flesh, or skin, of people. Similarly, in Matthew 16:17, "flesh and blood" denotes any human being.

**Parables:** Parables, *mashal or mashalim* (pl), in Hebrew use everyday words and images of life to express sublime and eternal truths. They were word pictures used by the ancient rabbis to teach and illustrate the unknown with what is known. Parables in both rabbinic and synoptic Gospel context were often connected to folklore culture. A parable was to generate a decisive response. The term *haggadah,* or storytelling, was used to communicate critical themes in their message.

**Personification:** Personification occurs when an object or concept is referred to as if it were a person. An example of this figurative language is seen in Proverbs, where Wisdom is personified as a woman: "Wisdom shouts in the street; she lifts her voice in the square" (1:20).

Figures of speech are extremely important in reading the Bible. Figures of speech and idioms within the biblical community were essential and should be taken into consideration when studying the Scriptures to avoid contextual misinterpretation.

Idioms, metaphors and parables are all significant when reading the Bible. Understanding them connects the reader in so many ways to time, place and event. Following the Spirit is critical and necessary for the believer; yet the need for study is also essential. We are to study to show ourselves approved unto God, not men—including ourselves. To rightly comprehend the word of truth, we must remove all modern-day trends and tendencies.

*Rabbinic Teaching Technique*

In addition to figures of speech there were also various rabbinic teaching styles. These are referred to as classic rabbinic techniques that utilized two types of discourse material. The first is known as *halakha*, and the second, *aggadah*, also *haggadah*; both were developed during the inter-testament period. Yeshua actively used aggadah when teaching the disciples; it was common knowledge within the biblical community.

**Halakha:** Halakha has a broad definition, but I will give the brief overall meaning. Halakha originates from a word meaning "to go" or "way." It is translated as the word *law*; it is anything that pertains to law, commandment, rule or instructions. It includes rulings on what to do and what not to do in a certain situation and the legal descriptions, prescriptions or decisions of the sages. Described simply, halakha is "the way to walk" or "the way to live." It deals with everyday issues in Judaic life. In Jewish thought halakha is "the path of life"; it takes the ordinary activities and sanctifies them.

**Aggadah:** Aggadah is also broad in definition; in short it is anything that is not halakha. Aggadah involves parables, legends, ethical statements, lore, stories, biblical theology, hermeneutics and exegesis of scripture. The commonly known aspects of aggadah are parables, teachings and the Midrash. Aggadah does not focus on the legalism of halakha; its focus is on relational ethical levels. Aggadah is about getting people to live morally right lives and bringing them closer to God. Yeshua used this style when teaching the disciples.

*Numerical System*

**Gematria:** The gematria is a system of calculating numerical value of Hebrew letters, words and phrases within a Hebrew text. Gematria is used to gain insight into concepts and explore the relationships between words and ideas. Because there is no numerical system within the language of Hebrew, letters represent numbers, and these numbers can convey a message within the written Hebrew texts.

Gematria uses numbers and should not be confused with numerology, though some relegate it to such a position. Numerology is speculative and arbitrary. Gematria on the other hand is a simple yet powerful method of understanding scriptural connections. There are several methods to calculate gematria, and understanding these systems has significant value. In the next chapter I will include an example that explains gematria as it relates to identity.

# Chapter Two:

# Truth/Falsehood

This book is about the armor of the Lord and how identity is woven into it to give life. Truth is necessary to having an awareness of one's true identity, so I want to share the gematria of "truth" and "falsehood."

Truth is *emet* in Hebrew. By simplest definition emet is "the all encompassing." It comes from an action word meaning to make firm or support. The opposite of this is a Hebrew word, *sheker*, which means a falsehood or lie. A lie is unable to stand because it does not carry the substance of what is all-encompassing. The Hebrew language is living, and the letters used to spell "truth" and "lie" express an active visual illustration to establish living principle.

**TRUTH — EMET — אֱמֶת**
**FALSEHOOD — SHEKER — שקר**

First I want to point out a characteristic of emet. Notice how each letter in the word rests flatly on the underline above; each is in line with the other. Now notice how the letters in sheker fall out of line with each other. The middle letter, *kof*, extends below the rest of the letters. Sheker conveys falsehood. It has a letter falling below the line, showing its inability to stand. When truth does not exist, nothing stands. When truth is absent in any situation, it will never stand. Every person must come to this realization in order to understand his or her divinely given identity.

As a scribe writing Hebrew letters I experience the hidden mysteries within the message of the Word. I say experience because everything about God is not only to be seen or known but also encountered so that we are united in Him through the experience. I want to share the gematria principle using the numerical language. As explained earlier, every Hebrew letter has a numerical value. Below I have given the gematria for emet and sheker to reveal the spiritual significance of what the words represent. Using the alphabet chart from the previous section (Illustration 1) we can find the numerical value of each letter and furnish deeper insight in the calculations.

**TRUTH: EMET — ת (400) מ (40) א (1)**

$400 + 40 + 1 = 441$ — 441 is reduced to 9 [4 + 4 + 1]

**FALSEHOOD: SHEKER — ר (200) ק (100) ש (300)**

$200 + 100 + 300 = 600$ — 600 is reduced to 6 [6 + 0 + 0]

Truth is reduced to nine, making it the ninth Hebrew letter, *tet*. Nine, according to the hermeneutic numerical principle, is the number for judgment. Tet symbolizes goodness in the Hebraic context. In Genesis 1 the Lord calls all that He made "good." This usage does not indicate something good in regard to its quality, decency, morality or pleasantness. (These definitions of good are useless at this point due to nothing yet being "bad" or inferior, immoral or unpleasant.) The term *good* in Genesis 1 is about something functioning as it was designed. Creation functions actively because of God's intention.

When the Lord called something into being, it came by His intention. A clearer way of seeing this is to see God's creation not as an invention but as His intention. "Good" is when all of creation is operating in the design of His intention; this is truth. Truth in connection with identity is the intention of the Creator, thus making it able to stand. If a lie attempts to become a marker for truth, it will fail because it lacks the intention of God.

Falsehood, on the other hand, when reduced to the smallest number is six; the sixth Hebrew letter is *vav*. Six, according to hermeneutic numerical principles, is the number for man. Vav symbolizes completion, redemption and transformation. Vav is also the "connector." Man is God's crowning creative moment endowed with the ability to comprehend the Creator. When man disobeyed God, the word between image and likeness and the Creator was broken, resulting in lost relationship. Adam did not "fall" so to speak in Genesis 3, but rather he turned away from his Creator. Sin is the result of this turning away. A sinner is a person who fails to fulfill who he or she is as the image and likeness of God. Sin is to fail at being who God designed us to be. Man went from tending to creation as master to toiling as a slave because of the covering of flesh and not the covering of God's Word. Falsehood against truth is the basis of man's continual struggle.

Deception will result in repeated futile cycles in the attempt to cover where truth is but just covered up. The destructive habits of a person are only broken through the grace given by God. Deception breaks and fragments the soul. Identity within the intention of God is the unbroken state of His Word. Identity is what God says about us and not what anything else may try to clothe us with.

The numerical difference between truth and falsehood is three (9 − 6 = 3). The number three symbolizes manifestation; it is the third Hebrew letter *gimmel*. Gimmel represents the kindness of God when He reveals Himself among creation. Exodus 34:6-7 gives us a description of God's lovingkindness. He proclaims His compassion, saying He is slow to anger and abounding in truth. John 3:16 is similarly well-known for displaying God's love for the world. God has always intended that we know who we are through Him only. As Creator nothing else can define us outside of Him.

Identity and truth are inseparable when it comes to humanity and even more so for believers in Yeshua. Identity often is communicated through cultural orientation, language, belief structures and the like. But for the sake of this book I will describe identity as "the function of God's image and likeness." Ask yourself how many faces you present to the world. How many times have you not been yourself in order to gain acceptance? Or how many lies have you lived at some point to get ahead? People in general want to be accepted as "good" people. Believers are not exempt from this thought. Most will say, "I am a good Christian," but is there such a thing as a "bad" Christian? Being in a relationship with God has nothing to do with being good or bad. To walk with the Lord is to know who you are regardless of external influences.

Identity will be either truth (Yeshua/salvation) or falsehood (Satan). Truth will bring identity as God intended; falsehood will bring incident. When truth is the point of origin, there is stability. When there is no truth, everything is unstable. To have an anointed mind is to be stable. Stability is to have an unwavering perspective according to God's intention. It is that oneness that Yeshua speaks of in John 14 and 17. James 1:7 speaks of the double mind. Corruption of truth yields a double mind because it lacks God's wisdom, which is the will of God at all times.

Truth pervades the human desire of wanting to be loved and accepted by the beloved. I love a definition of destiny my Eema (Mommie Paula) gave me. She said, "Destiny is every breath a person takes in becoming who they were created to be." I have learned since first hearing this that humanity is the image and likeness of the Father of us all. He has given His Word, and in turn we have life. We are good because we function according to divine intention. I don't have to invent anything that validates who I am.

God's kingdom consists of all those who identify themselves as part of the body of Yeshua. It is His name whereby believers are baptized into His body and returned to their original identity. John 14 gives a wonderful explanation of what it means to be in Him: We are to believe we are in Him, not about Him. Just as we were in Adam, so are we in Yeshua. Believers have received a covering that serves as armor.

Language and culture are entwined. Language conveys culture, and culture conveys the values by which we perceive ourselves and our place in the world. The Word of God is living and requires relationship. Hebrew is essential to experiencing who we are to our heavenly Father. The language of the Bible is inseparable from the community of believers within the kingdom of God. As sons and daughters of the Most High God our distinctiveness is the restoration of the unity we have as image and likeness. Believers in salvation are given the gift of what was in the garden where it all began.

# Chapter Three:

# In the Beginning

The beginning as recorded in the Bible reveals God's plan for all of creation. Every believer must maintain a clear perception of where life started in order to fully realize the plan of salvation. Genesis is the book of origins. It can be considered the seed of the entire Bible; its first chapter is the summation of all we know regarding the created world and humanity, and an in-depth study of this book can take a lifetime.

> In the beginning God created the heavens and the earth (Genesis 1:1).

בראשית ברא אלהים את השמים ואת הארץ

B'reishit bara Elohim et hashamayim ve'et ha'arets.

B'reishit speaks of "in the beginning." This passage of Scripture is not an historical account of creation as most believe but a charter of creation's duty by the command and sovereignty of God. At the beginning creation was filled with blessing. Everything the earth receives from the Creator is a blessing. The Jewish text, the Chumash, records Genesis 1 as "In the beginning of God's creating the heavens and the earth."[2] This beginning is a sequential testimony of creative events that culminated with the creation of man. In this process of creation God establishes His sovereignty over the universe. In its fullness creation is the "covering" for the Word of God. Prior to the separation of man from God, all of creation was at an exalted state uncursed. Our current state of comprehension cannot be used to describe the original state of anything as we know it today; it would be too "low."

> "I am the Alpha and the Omega," says the Lord God, "who is and who was and who is to come, the Almighty" (Revelation 1:8).

> "I am the Alpha and the Omega, the first and the last, the beginning and the end" (Revelation 22:13).

Yeshua was the Word referred to during God's creation. Revelation uses the Greek letters *alpha* and *omega*, but in Hebrew it would be *aleph* and *tav*, the two letters underlined below in Genesis 1:1.

בראשית ברא אלהים **את** השמים ואת הארץ

B'reishit bara Elohim **et** hashamayim ve'et ha'arets.

Hiding within this opening are the letters *aleph* and *tav*, the first and last letters of the Hebrew alphabet. As discussed earlier, the letters of the Hebrew alphabet are fundamental units, decrees that bring creation into being. The alphabetical succession is the totality described in Yeshua. When the aleph and tav are present, everything that is destined is absolute. The letters *aleph* and *tav* serve as the all-inclusive work of God. It is essential to the believers of the Christian faith to

52

have the greater reality of who Yeshua is as the Word. Aleph and tav represent the complete and accomplished work of Yeshua in the first line of Genesis, before all things.

In the cycle of creation there is always a return to the point of origin. The Lord is constant and always the same. He is ever present in His creation, including man. What draws every soul back to the essence of the Creator is this invisible presence that resides in every person.

The greatest testimony we have as witnesses to this unseen presence is our obedience to the Word of God. Dominion is man's destiny as outlined by God's perfection. When I speak of perfection, it is not referring to faultlessness or flawlessness. Maturing of the soul is the preparation to eternal restoration in God. If we fail to know who we are, then we fail at knowing to whom we belong; so where are we going? Perfection can perhaps be understood as mature personal integrity including the responsibility of free will.

Psalm 119:89 says, "Forever, O Lord, thy word is settled in heaven." Jewish tradition reads this psalm as praise of the spiritual significance of the letters themselves. A more literal translation of the Hebrew would read, "Forever, Lord, Your word stands firm in heaven." The "stands firm," according to tradition, refers to Genesis 1:6, where God said, "Let there be a firmament." What's being referred to by this allusion is the belief that God's Spirit or "breath" is manifest.

The identity of every person is immense, and it becomes immeasurable in light of embracing who we are in the Lord. Each Hebrew letter reveals how we are built into the word God has spoken. He calls all by name, and it is in the name of Yeshua that all names live, move and have a being. Believers must know who they are in name as well as HaShem (the Name) who calls all.

*Being Adam*

To connect ourselves to the kingdom of God, we must examine who we are in God's plan. At the time of creation everything was given a name and function so that God's intention would be seen. When a person is born he unconsciously begins life at the point of earthly entry; but humanity truly entered into the earth realm by the will of God at the time of creation.

> Then God said, "Let Us make man in Our image, according to Our likeness; and let them rule over the fish of the sea and over the birds of the sky and over the cattle and over all the earth, and over every creeping thing that creeps on the earth." God created man in His own image, in the image of God He created him; male and female He created them. God blessed them; and God said to them, "Be fruitful and multiply, and fill the earth, and subdue it; and rule over the fish of the sea and over the birds of the sky and over every living thing that moves on the earth" (Genesis 1:26-28).

The image and likeness of God are where we begin. It is the character of God that brings about His nature. Adam is the Creator's highest opinion of who He is in creation. Adam is both male and female. He is the divine agent that represents divine authority. Adam is the vessel designed to carry not only the breath of God but also the comprehension of God's breath.

When Adam was made, both male and female resided in him. Genesis 1:27 says, "God created man in His own image, in the image of God He created him; male and female He created them." Adam is not a "male." Adam is male and female; he is two in one flesh. In the mind of God male and female exist as one. When the male and female are one in covenant, they return to that place of creation where both were one with their Father. For every male there is a female because both were in the mind of God as Adam. It is by divine planning that they are to follow the order of life to reconnect in the natural. It is in real relationship with the Creator Himself that each male and female are established, and later they come together as one flesh. When two people are married, it is more than a wedding; it is the manifestation of the covenant of all covenants. People don't marry each other; they together as one come into covenant with the Lord.

God established covenant with Adam in the union of male and female. When God blew the breath of life, both male and female received it at the same time; they are equal in image and likeness. In the order and function of God, however, He places male as the one responsible in the covenant. Covenant is by divine design. When separation from God, the source of all identity, takes place, then the invention of acceptance forms and totally distorts the original plan of God. In Adam male and female are one in mind and heart, and together they submit all strength in service of God.

Adam was made a living soul, but his difference from creation was his identity as being created in God's image and likeness. The next section will be linguistically technical, but it is indispensable for the comprehension of image and likeness.

In Genesis 2:7, which describes the formation of Adam, the Hebrew *va-yitzer* is used; it often also is used to describe the work of a potter (*yotzer*). After God breathed the breath of life into Adam, he became a living being (*nephesh chayyah*). The breath of life (*nishmat hayyim*) is a distinct life given directly by God to Adam apart from that given to all other living creatures.

The word *nephesh* is the word that's often translated "soul." Genesis 2:7 is best understood as describing Adam as a "living soul" rather than a "living being." In other words, God did not give man a soul; man *is* a soul.

Adam's soul within Hebraic context does not align with what Christian theology conveys. The Hebrew word for spirit is *ruach* and is also the word for wind or breath. Some biblical scholars err in thinking that God's breathing life into man gave man a spirit, which made him distinct from animals. But the word *ruach* is not used here. The Hebrew in Genesis 2:7 can be transliterated as "And [God] breathed into his nostrils a breath of life. Man [thus] became a living creature." Mechanically translated, this would read, "And He exhaled in his nostrils a breath of life and the human existed for a being of life."[3] When I say mechanical, I am referring to a very literal translation arranged using English grammar. While ruach is inferred, it is not imparted into man in the text. The word used is connected to *n'shamah* (translated here as "breath") and has the same meaning as *nephesh* in rabbinic literature.

Genesis 7:21-22 transliterated says:

Vayigva kol-basar haromes al-ha'arets ba'of uvabe-hemah uvachayah uvechol-hasherets hashorets al-ha'arets vechol ha'adam. Kol asher nishmat-ruach chayim be'apav mikol asher becharavah metu.

All flesh that walked the earth perished: birds, live-stock, wild beasts, and every lower animal that swarmed on the land, as well as every human being. Everything on dry land whose life was sustained by breathing died.

The phrase "everything. . .whose life was sustained by breathing" is, literally, "all that has a breath of the spirit of life," or "all that has in it a life-giving breath." *N'shamah ruach chayyim*, or "breath of spirit of life," and *n'shamah chayyim* are interchangeable, which suggests man did receive the ruach when God breathed into him. Adam is given divine identity, not a carnal identity. It is vital to see that everything prior to Adam's walking away from God cannot be perceived "post sin." Nothing from Genesis 3 on can even attempt to define, describe or defend what "life" was given when God breathed into Adam.

The language used in regard to all living things in Genesis 7:21-22 is the same language used in regard to man in Genesis 2:7. Birds and beasts and all living things appear to have received *n'shamah ruach chayyim* at some point in order for them to have life; but what made Adam distinct was being in the image and likeness of God.

*Image and Likeness*

> He is the image of the invisible God, the firstborn of all creation. For by Him all things were created, both in the heavens and on earth, visible and invisible, whether thrones or dominions or rulers or authori- ties—all things have been created through Him and for Him. He is before all things, and in Him all things hold together (Colossians 1:15-17).

Genesis 1 says, "And God saw that it was good." "Good," again, relates to something functioning within the intention of God's design; it is not in this context "upright" or "all right." Good is the evidence of God's intention through His percep- tion. Light operated within the nature and design endowed by the Creator Himself. The first good to have a purpose was light. Light is declared to be good in Genesis 1:4, and its survival was dependent upon the will and approval of God.

Colossians 1:13-14 says, "For He rescued us from the domain of darkness, and transferred us to the kingdom of His beloved Son, in whom we have redemption, the forgiveness of sins." As children of the light we are perceived by God as good. The function of a born-again person is in Yeshua, who is deemed the light of the world and the life of men. Yeshua, as the head, has given every believer communion with the Creator. We have been given the opportunity to walk once again with the Creator and return to true divine identity, man's greatest destiny.

> He is also head of the body, the church; and He is the beginning, the firstborn from the dead, so that He Himself will come to have first place in every-thing. For it was the Father's good pleasure for all the fullness to dwell in Him, and through Him to reconcile all things to Himself, having made peace through the blood of His cross; through Him, I say, whether things on earth or things in heaven. And although you were formerly alienated and hostile in mind, engaged in evil deeds, yet He has now recon-ciled you in His fleshly body through death, in order to present you before Him holy and blameless and beyond reproach—if indeed you continue in the faith firmly established and steadfast, and not moved away from the hope of the gospel that you have heard, which was proclaimed in all creation under heaven (Colossians 1:8-23a).

Our nature and character are not based on any earthly defini-tion or explanation but on the ruling of God. The dominion of man comes from the image and likeness of God. "Image," in Hebrew, is *tzelem* which also means "shadow." Tzelem does not refer to the physical aspect of man but the "intel-lectual" aspect of man. Man has been given the capacity to perceive through divine intellect God and His wisdom. Tzelem is the reflection of God. God's Word is inclu-sive of patterns regarding reflection. The tabernacle in the wilderness, the temple in Jerusalem and even Yeshua the Amidah were patterns alluding to heaven. [The Amidah was central to Jewish prayer; it was established during the time of Ezra when Jews were required to pray three times a day; today it consists of four times: *shacharit* (morning), *mincha* (afternoon), *maariv* (evening) and *mussaf* (additional). The word *Amidah* literally means "standing," because it is recited while standing. It is also known as *Shemoneh Esrei*, meaning "eighteen," because it originally consisted of eighteen blessings.] What many Christians refer to as the Lord's Prayer is actually an abbreviated version of the Amidah taught by Yeshua. The Amidah in the Gospels speaks of heaven being reflected on earth as God's kingdom and will come forth. Mankind through the revelation of God's Word has the ability to reflect the light of God. To have a reflection there must be light. Mankind was given this light (see Matthew 5:13-15; John 1:8-10, 8:11-13, 9:4-6, 12:45-47; 2 Corinthians 4:3-5). As the image and likeness of God mankind was to reflect the Creator by being fruitful, multiplying, subduing and having dominion. At the point of God's blessing Adam as male and female their formation was not yet in place; therefore the "fruitfulness" was not solely flesh.

The word *demut* (likeness) is rooted in the word *dam*, which means "blood." One descended from the blood of another often resembles the one descended from. *Damah* means "to resemble" and is the root for *demut*, which means "a resemblance" or "to be like something else in action or appearance." Man, "Adam," is divine thought able to recognize divine wisdom while the Word of God serves as man's spiritual DNA.

In Genesis 3:9 God calls to Adam, "Where are you?" God is all-knowing and had not lost man, but something was no longer present in Adam. God is asking, "Where is the light I created you to be that makes seeing Me possible?" and, "Where is the illumination you had of Me as your

Creator that set you apart from the rest of creation?" What was lost when Adam stopped walking with God was the light, or his revelation of God. We don't see light. Light is what makes seeing possible. It was the light or the revelation of God within Adam that made seeing God possible. It is this same light that speaks or causes things to come into being by making seeing possible.

Adam was with the Lord and was able to speak in accordance to the revelation, the light of God. Adam had the light of God, and in this state dominion and power were in their purest form. In this state there was no darkness or corruption through the law or nature of sin. Light is so important because it is the original existence of man. In the garden, light was the covering just as flesh later becomes the covering. Adam's uniqueness as a speaking spirit made him so powerful in the role of God's agent that God gave him the ability and power to name the animals. Just as God separates light from darkness and dry land from water, this biblical text affirms that humans—created in the image of God—may seek to bring order to our chaotic and dynamic world through the process of naming. The act of naming confers leadership and authority.

> Out of the ground the Lord God formed every beast of the field and every bird of the sky, and brought them to the man to see what he would call them; and whatever the man called a living creature, that was its name. The man gave names to all the cattle, and to the birds of the sky, and to every beast of the field (Genesis 2:19-20).

It was the act of seeking something other than the Creator that caused the demise of Adam. Another identity was introduced because another "word" was persuasively suggestive. God told Adam the day he ate of the Tree of Knowledge of Good and Evil he would surely die. It is clear that Adam did not die a physical death in Genesis 3. The word that Adam had been given was broken. The word being broken does not imply being destroyed but a breach in creation between God and man. The broken word was the act of violence that caused the separation and darkness of Adam.

God's Spirit in man darkened because of knowledge, and man leaned to himself. Contrary to what some theologians believe, Adam had a "born-again" experience; but it was the opposite of how the term is usually defined. Just as a person's spiritual eyes are opened by the revelation of Yeshua, so is their spirit-man again illuminated through quickening. Adam's awareness of self darkened his spiritual self; it is the reverse of our experience. All that we are as man is "self awareness." As a born-again man we return to "God awareness." Attending church service and saying "I'm a Christian" or having some ordination and receiving some "spiritual" authority title are not the evidence of salvation. Prior to Genesis 2 Adam was the government of God ruling creation. In Yeshua (salvation) God's government is established once and for all. The authority of Yeshua is now the covering believers are to walk in.

When Adam disobeyed God, sin (flesh) became the result of disobedience. Sin at the most basic level is to wander. Sin is the failure to fulfill the intended destiny set by God. The true salvation encounter should never be individualistic or self-pursuing. Man has a godly heritage and a sovereign inheritance. Have you ever asked, "What, then, was lost in the garden?" It was the covering or the position of authority. Mankind lost sight of their kind. Adam was the name given to mankind. This name by function became our identity as man. Without a name or an identity there is no authority; without authority there is no dominion. Adam went from tending, a sign of stewardship, to toiling, a sign of slavery. No one enjoys being enslaved; yet sin confines a person in his or her flesh. The nature of sin is to produce slaves, while the character of slaves of sin is to produce the fruit of sin. In either case both are against God and His desire for creation.

Mankind traded the place of power and dominion for the domination of knowledge, something that is not true power. In Genesis 3 Eve fails at that moment to recognize she is already like God. The greatest deception is mankind failing to see who they are already. More often than not we are deceived by our own will. For some reason Eve's revelation of God was not enough. A false identity is the culprit in many cases of deception, for both believers and unbelievers.

Salvation is what covers our nakedness so we are not ashamed and will not attempt to hide from our Creator. Remember that in Genesis 3:21 the Lord Himself covers Adam. "The Lord God made garments of skin for Adam and his wife, and clothed them."

In order to have proper perception of man's soul it must always remain a part of God. The covering of Adam both male and female was the Word of God. Their nakedness was not "flesh" as in human skin as some would suppose when thinking of their nakedness. If this was so then why would God need to give them garments of skin? The one thing that must be taken into consideration when comprehending creation is that there is nothing that means "no–thing" that can be used to define, describe or depend upon concerning the condition of creation after Adam's walking away. After that ill-fated act all comprehension is all knowledge, the very fruit mankind was not to partake of. What we see today as creation is a cursed condition; therefore redemption was crucial.

The nakedness of the original couple was not their ability to see themselves as naked in "flesh" form, but in the removing of revelation by the covering of knowledge as to who they were but even more so who God is. God covers them not with animal "skin" but with His Word. God covers Adam with the Lamb that was sacrificed before the foundation of the world.

And all the inhabitants of the earth will fall down in adoration and pay him homage, everyone whose name has not been recorded in the Book of Life of the Lamb that was slain [in sacrifice] from the foundation of the world (Revelation 13:8 AMP).

In the fullness of time the Word becomes flesh in the likeness of sin whereby salvation redeems or brings mankind back to God. Yeshua as mediator (the Word of God) reconciles and restores. God redeems His Word. The body of man returns to the place of creation in the Creator. Until the time of redeeming of the Word, flesh (sin) was the veil of separation.

So also we while we were children were held in bondage under the elemental things of the world. But when the fullness of the time came, God sent forth His Son, born of a woman, born under the Law, so that He might redeem those who were under the Law, that we might receive the adoption as sons (Galatians 4:3-5).

The law of sin is the bondage that separated because of the broken word in the garden. Salvation is the accomplished word where nothing is missing or is no longer broken. Yeshua as the Word returns to the Father mankind and all creation accomplished and fulfilled.

By faith we understand that the worlds were prepared by the word of God, so that what is seen was not made out of things which are visible. By faith Abel offered to God a better sacrifice than Cain, through which he obtained the testimony that he was righteous, God testifying about his gifts, and through faith, though he is dead, he still speaks (Hebrews 11: 3-4).

The seed of the woman is immediately seen with the birth of Cain and Abel. There had to be fruit of good and evil. Both Abel and Cain are the results of knowledge of good and evil, Abel representing "good" and Cain representing evil.

Our spiritual man, once quickened in the new birth process, is the enlarging of God's Spirit within us. We have tremendous potential as the likeness and image of God. Our ability to embrace God comes when we respond as the image and likeness of God when He reveals Himself within us. As believers in Yeshua, when our behavior is not in accordance with the Lord's precepts, we have betrayed our Creator and Father. Even more we have betrayed ourselves and fallen short of our true potential; this is sin.

Identity as it relates to light can be summed up as God redeeming all back to their place in God. This place is not so much a consigned location but the revelation of God by God. The fullness of this Word is Yeshua and His authority. As the beginning, ending, the first, the last and the all-encompassing One, Yeshua is more than Lord and Savior. He is the restored Word which was lost in the garden in the beginning. As the light the revelation is made available to reconcile proper identity back to man in order to return dominion within God's kingdom.

With a restored relationship comes a connection in name. I will conclude this chapter by giving further explanation of light by using one of the names for God, El Olam. El Olam is The Everlasting God or Eternal God. This name is commonly recognized as being without beginning or end; therefore it means beyond all we as humanity can invent, imagine or choose to ignore. This definition seems to intend well; yet it falls short in describing the relationship between Adam and God.

The Hebrew word *olam* ("everlasting") is seen as without end—but how can this be when God is without beginning?

Olam to the ancient Hebrews was time that is hidden from the present. The ancient Hebrews did not define olam as without end. It is related to the horizon. A horizon is where the sun or sky touches the earth or water in the distance. We can see the horizon, but not what is beyond it. Olam is that place where we cannot see from where we are standing. Olam is the direction where light gathers. Olam is the inability to comprehend within human perceptions. What's on the other side of the horizon cannot be seen from where a person stands, but this doesn't say there is nothing there. Olam is seeing beyond what natural eyes are able to see.

Kingdom identity must connect to the origin. This origin is in the person where salvation (Yeshua) is the revelation of God as the light which makes seeing God possible once again.

*The Naming of Adam*

The entrance of sin into the garden was the separation point between God and man. When God says in Genesis 1:26, "Let Us make man in Our image, according to Our likeness," Adam experienced covenant with his Creator. There are two aspects of the name Adam:

1.  Aleph — the first letter in the word for man, "Adam"
2.  Dam — the Hebrew word for blood

Before I continue I am placing a disclaimer regarding my relationship with Adonai. I live within the perimeters of God's Word for my belief structure. Salvation completely rests in Mashiach, the power and authority of Yeshua. There is nothing outside of this. Yet the fullness of God's Word is far more than just sixty-six canonized books structured by men. I will share some things which may be foreign, but they reveal greater insight into God's overall purpose for all creation. All of creation, not just mankind, has been redeemed. Yeshua studied and utilized the rabbinic literature and the schools of thought of the day which must be taken into consideration.

The gematria system illuminates spiritual significance of the name Adam as it relates to God. God is represented by the first Hebrew letter, *aleph*. It is God the Creator, an unfathomable mystery of unity and harmony. Aleph has a numerical value of one. It is the first prime number, which signifies a beginning. Aleph is one of two consonants in the Hebrew language that cannot be pronounced. It is always silent, indicating the qualities of being hidden, incomprehensible, unexplainable and infinite.

The word *aleph* in the ancient Hebrew pictograph is the head of a bull signifying the headship; royalty. It symbolizes the beginning of everything in the universe. All had its origin within and from God. Aleph is related to the word *aluph*, which means "master." This all alludes to the sovereignty of God. When viewed at the basic level, aleph carries the Tetragrammaton and has a numerical value of twenty-six. The Tetragrammaton is the "word with four letters" and is the usual reference to the Hebrew name for God, spelled as: י (yud) ה (hei) ו (vav) ה (hei) (reading right to left) = YHVH. It is the distinctive personal name of the God of Israel. If we were to break this down to its smallest value it would be the number eight. Aleph conceals YHVH within the letter structure itself. The four letters numerically are the same with the appearance of two י (yud) valued as the tenth letter plus the slanted ו (vav) valued as the sixth letter. The letters within aleph, when added, have the same value as YHVH.

In calculating the holy name YHVH as a number, we see that yud (10) + hei (5) + vav (6) + hei (5) = 26. The smallest form of this is eight (which we get by adding 2 + 6 = 8). The number eight is the number denoting beginning.[4] The eighth letter is *chet* and symbolizes divine grace and life.

The Lord's grace and life have been His sole purpose from the very beginning.

The second aspect of Adam (ם – ד – א) is the Hebrew word *dam*. Dam is cognate to the word for likeness, *demut*. Dam is spelled right to left, *dalet* and the final *mem* (ם – ד). The letter *aleph* by itself is "ah" and is usually silent. It is the element of air, or breath. Adam can be seen as the blood with the breath of life. Adam is literally the A-DAM or first blood, first life. The word *Adam* reversed is *moda*, which in the ancient Hebrew means "friend."

Redemption is the reversal of the effects of sin, which caused man to lose a place of friendship with his Creator. Yet even in the naming of man the plan of salvation came through the blood, which carries life. Adam as moda is God's friend, redeemed through the forgiveness of sin by the blood of salvation, Yeshua.

"Blood" has a gematria numerical value of 604. Dam spelled uses the letters *dalet* 4 + the final *mem* 600 (600 + 4 to the smallest point is $6 + 0 + 0 + 4 = 10 = 1 + 0 = 1$). This is the same numerical value of the sacred four-letter name for God, YHVH. It is seen first as the Hebrew letter *aleph* (א) represented as the first (1). Within the letter *aleph* as previously explained carries two yuds and a slanted vav. The numerical value of YHVH is twenty-six as the only One. Adam is the essential agent to the divine essence. Setting salvation aside, man has always been destined to be spiritual and eternal.

The Hebrew word for man is *ish*. It comes from the word for fire, *eish*. Man is unique among all living beings because of his ability to dominate, attain wisdom and develop culture. Fire is seen as strength; it is the pressing that brings about illumination. It is represented by the concept of initiative, enthusiasm and lust. The Hebrew word for woman is *ishah*. As Adam's companion, she is literally a helper to him.

The presence of godliness in humanity is expressed when the letters *yud* and *hei* are revealed in their names. The letter *yud* is contained in the word *man*; the letter *hei* is in *woman*. The combination of these two letters spelled the divine name Yah. They are the tenth and fifth letters of the alphabet; yet when combined to the smallest number they become six, the number for man ($10 + 5 = 15 = 1 + 5 = 6$). Man, Adam as male and female, was created on the sixth day.

> Then the Lord God formed man of dust from the ground, and breathed into his nostrils the breath of life; and man became a living being (Genesis 2:7).

This verse paraphrased could read, "God breathed into man, and he became a living soul." God's breathing into us is His exhaling. In this exhalation the power of God by His will went into the intended dwelling place, Adam.

We breathe by inhaling and exhaling. Something is taken in and something released; we respire. When God exhaled He drew from nothing to inhale. So, then, if God exhaled, would it not make sense to see Him as now inhaling by bringing us back to Him?

As believers in Yeshua, when we surrender in Him we are exhaling and God is now inhaling. Yeshua is the truth and the only one that can put back what was broken in the garden: the Father's Word. It is not just the fact that sin entered in but that the eternal Word of God was broken in the garden. Sin is the lie that stripped us of our identity. If there is a propensity to bend or lie, then there is the possibility of breaking. If there is a propensity to stand erect, then there is the provision to be elevated. Integrity is the state of being complete or unbroken. It is the condition whereby wholeness is absolute. *Shalom* ("peace") is the unbroken Word of God. Every person belongs to the nature of a holy God.

# Chapter Four:

# Born Again

So also it is written, "The first man, Adam, became a living soul." The last Adam became a life-giving spirit. The spiritual is not first, however, but the natural; then the spiritual. The first man is from the earth, earthy; the second man is from heaven. As is the earthy, so also are those who are earthy; and as is the heavenly, so also are those who are heavenly. Just as we have borne the image of the earthy, we will also bear the image of the heavenly (1 Corinthians 15:45-49).

Yeshua said to Nicodemus in John 3, "Unless one is born again, he cannot see the kingdom of God." Puzzled by this, Nicodemus, though a ruler of the Pharisees, showed that man's knowledge was still not able to grasp spiritual revelation. Yeshua shows God's love by explaining to Nicodemus:

That which is born of the flesh is flesh, and that which is born of the Spirit is spirit. "Do not be amazed that I said to you, 'You must be born again.' The wind blows where it wishes and you hear the sound of it,

but do not know where it comes from and where it is
going; so is everyone who is born of the Spirit.
Spiritually speaking, a born-again believer is given the new
name Yeshua, who is the life-giving Spirit. To a learned
Jewish person such as Nicodemus, the born-again idiom was
easily understood through *mikvah*. Mikvah was a ritual bath
used for ritual immersion. The word *mikvah* literally means
a "collection," specifically a collection of water. The process
of being born again was not known to the Jews of Yeshua's
day as it is to Christians today.

The concept of purity and impurity as mandated by the
Torah and applied within Jewish life is unique; it has no
parallel or equivalent in this postmodern age. Perhaps that
is why it is difficult for the contemporary mind to relate to
the notion and view it as relevant. In ancient times ritual
purity and impurity were central to worshipping God. It was
required that people immerse themselves prior to entering
the temple; without immersion it would have been impossible to enter the temple, a place to meet God.

When speaking to Nicodemus, Yeshua is referring to
the ritual of *tevilah*. Tevilah is full body washing through
immersion in a mikvah. Tevilah is connected to the Hebrew
word *tikvah,* which means "hope," or, literally, "that which
gathers together." Mikvah literally means a "gathering
together," a "collection" or a "reservoir." Mikvah is a purification process to correct a condition of ritual impurity and
restore the impure to a state of ritual purity.

Mikvah parallels Christian baptism. It is being purified in
order to enter into the presence of God; the cleansed condition by being immersed—"the state of being one" in Yeshua.
Being pure or impure is ritually fit or unfit as it related to
temple worship. It should not be viewed as sinless or sinful.

All washing (immersion) during the time of Yeshua was connected to the person having fulfilled what was required to enter into the temple (the presence of God).

In ancient times Israel lived in the desert where water was critical to survival. When water was found it served as a symbol for hope.

Therefore my heart is glad and my glory [my inner self] rejoices; my body too shall rest and confidently dwell in safety, for You will not abandon me to Sheol [the place of the dead], neither will You suffer Your holy one to see corruption (Psalm 16:9-10 AMP).

The word *rest* in Psalm 16 is tikvah. It gives the assurance of life through regeneration. A closer analysis of Yeshua's conversation with Nicodemus brings to light the "born-again" analogy. Within Hebraic thought the mikvah mainly personifies the womb as opposed to a grave as commonly taught in Christian belief for water baptism. The fetus is totally immersed in what is known as a water sac; the medical term is an amniotic sac. Immersion was extremely important in biblical times because it was symbolic of returning to God.

Immersion indicates the abandonment of one form of existence to embrace one infinitely higher. It is believed in Jewish tradition that the person is stripped of all power and influence during immersion. It is a moment of total reliance and complete resignation of control. In giving up power, the immersed Jew signals a desire to achieve oneness with the source of all life, to return to a unity with God. In keeping with this theme, immersion in the mikvah is described not only in terms of purification, revitalization and rejuvenation but also as rebirth. Nicodemus understood Yeshua meant the immersion into life was not a death but a change of status, a new beginning, just as when a baby is born.

Yeshua is the gateway to cleansing and restoration. To be placed in Him is to be placed where Adam was with the Father prior to the entrance of sin. He speaks of abiding in Him, not around Him. This abiding is unity with the Father through His Word, Yeshua—salvation. Ephesians 4:5 states, "One Lord, one faith, one baptism," or immersion, and speaks of the unification through regeneration of the spirit. When Paul wrote this, he was aware that there were many immersions within Judaism; but he was referring to the immersion into Mashiach, the placement in the body of Yeshua through the Spirit of God. Yeshua, by the function of His name, brings the character and nature of His Father, giving life. This life is spiritual which is quickened to the covenant between God and mankind, the covenant of fruitfulness, multiplicity, dominion and subduing.

*Yeshua's Character*

Throughout the Bible God has always wanted His image and likeness to manifest as the sons and daughters. In John 14–17 Yeshua repeatedly says, "If you believe in Me." He refers not to the belief that He existed and was a real person but to the actual realization that we are inside Him. We are baptized into His body. We are to abide in Yeshua. We live, move and have a being, not a doing, in Yeshua. There is one mikvah, baptism, immersion into Him. In Yeshua there is one faithfulness, His. There is one Spirit by which we live and that lives in us.

> Truly, truly, I say to you, he who believes in Me, the works that I do, he will do also; and greater works than these he will do; because I go to the Father.

Whatever you ask in My name, that will I do, so that the Father may be glorified in the Son. If you ask Me anything in My name, I will do it. If you love Me, you will keep My commandments (John 14:12-15).

A name in Hebraic thinking is also reputation. The name of a person was representative of actual character. So to say, "God is my Father," or, "Yeshua is my Lord," yet not bear the fruit of what these names mean is to take these names in vain. When you fail to live in a manner that embodies the Spirit of the Lord, you are taking His name for granted in vain by not setting your life apart and living unto Him, according to His Word.

The first followers of Yeshua had an advantage in having an identity as a people in covenant with the one true God. The first believers as the nation of Israel understood the importance of separation. As a chosen nation Israel is the recorded history that testifies to its witnessing of God. Today believers in Yeshua are to serve as the witness to God's Word by how we live separated unto the Father.

When we ask in His name, we are to be in the character of who He is. Yeshua's purpose was to bring mankind back to that place within God, where mankind was fully protected and able to perceive all things as God perceives. The name of Yeshua is the foundation of man's identity. It is in Him that believers are immersed, cleansed and made whole.

The world around us is built upon words of advertisement, media and other intruding influences. If a believer is not established in God's kingdom, his or her identity will develop from the external rather than the internal. If the world is speaking, where is it getting its words? Satan is called the god of this world in 2 Corinthians 4:4; it is he who speaks through the world. "Buy this! Live here! Wear this! Eat that! Drive!" and on and on and on.

In his continuous message Satan constantly veils humanity's sense of original identity by emphasizing the what, the where, the when, the how and the who. God's kingdom is not affected by the world, and neither should the identity of the believer be persuaded by it. We are not to be driven by worldly means to establish God's kingdom.

True kingdom identity never conflicts with the nature of the Father who is in all. Identity that is derived from the world is stolen by fads and trends, here today, gone tomorrow. The community of believers must rule by identity, since this is what was taken in the beginning. One enemy attacks in many ways, but the body of Yeshua is the armor that protects against the warfare of Satan. The connection between the believer's identity and the armor of the Lord is in the function of salvation. Believers bear who they are in the name (reputation) of Yeshua as the light of the world.

For You are our Father, though Abraham does not know us and Israel does not recognize us, You, O Lord, are our Father, our Redeemer from of old is Your name (Isaiah 63:16).

# Chapter Five:

# What Is Armor?

Armor, in a general sense, is for protection, not for use as a weapon. The purpose of armor is protective. Armor is intended to defend its wearer from intentional harm in combat and military engagements and is usually associated with soldiers. Armor has been used throughout history, beginning with hides and leather and bone, before progressing to bronze and eventually steel during the Roman Era.

The Roman government did not require armor. The amount of armor depended on the wealth and rank of the soldier or his patron. An ordinary foot soldier would have the basic protection of a leather breastplate and shield, in addition to a sword. Armor was something that served the soldier; it could mean life or death.

> Finally, be strong in the Lord and in the strength of His might. Put on the full armor of God, so that you will be able to stand firm against the schemes of the devil. For our struggle is not against flesh and blood, but against the rulers, against the powers, against the world forces of this darkness, against the spiritual forces of wickedness in the heavenly places. Therefore, take up the full armor of God, so that you

will be able to resist in the evil day, and having done everything, to stand firm (Ephesians 6:10-13).

Paul had the opportunity to observe many Roman soldiers fully equipped from head to toe. Rome's power came from its well-trained and well-equipped military force. Roman soldiers were skilled in strategy, weaponry, defense and understanding of the enemy. Using the Roman soldier's armor as a visual example, Paul describes the armor of God in Ephesians as both a defense against attack and an offensive weapon.

If anyone had firsthand knowledge of Roman weaponry, it would have been Paul, due to his numerous encounters with Roman law and frequent imprisonments. Paul's observations were critical during the domination and persecution of the Romans. He was showing the believers of the day who they were despite the oppressive Roman rule. Though a war was being waged against the body of believers, the believers were not sent into battle without the proper covering.

*Living Armor*

Do this, knowing the time that it is already the hour for you to awaken from sleep; for now salvation is nearer to us than when we believed. The night is almost gone, and the day is near. Therefore let us lay aside the deeds of darkness and put on the armor of light (Romans 13:11-12).

In his letter Paul encourages believers to put on the armor of light and behave properly. The believer's battle is not fleshly battle, because "the weapons of our warfare are not carnal," according to 2 Corinthians 10:4. The culture within the kingdom of God is based on two things: behavior and values. Behavior is defined as the outward manifestation of an inward control. Values on the other hand are desires, or those things that carry worth. Our behavior can be set based on the things we believe have worth. When behavior and values are combined, identity is present.

The armor for the born-again believer extends much further than understanding the physical armor. Divine armor is divine protection by divine identity. Divine armor is the power within the Lord Yeshua himself. The battle truly is not ours but Yeshua's. The "born-again" experience is a spiritual awakening, and, according to Ephesians 6:10, the battle is spiritual as well. If the war is spiritual, then would not the armor be also?

In Genesis 3 we see the account of Adam's feeble attempt to cover himself after his disobedience. Adam attempted to cover nakedness with inapt material. Adam lost the illumination and revelation of who he was and tried to fix the situation by leaning to what he had, knowledge of good and evil.

The believer's armor referred to in Ephesians 6, though drawn from Roman armor, is living and has an identity. It is what clothes us and makes us righteous. It is a fortress in which we can find refuge; it is our defense. The armor of the Lord is the hiding place where nothing can find us to accuse or condemn us. Collectively the armor and weapons for every believer are actively engaging—not independently but intra-dependently.

In order to gain a deeper understanding of the identity of armor and the power we have in the armor of the Lord we must look at the armor as living and not some inanimate object. Why would the body of Yeshua, a living community jointly fitted together, need physical armor for a spiritual battle? This is not to negate the analogies of Paul's message, but if one can put on something, then one can take it off. The armor is not a thing. The armor is in essence the person of Yeshua. He is the covering for all who are in Him. Each piece of the armor is designed to reveal the function and character of the one it embodies.

In the beginning when man was first created, the full revelation of God was Adam's light. This light was the armor that protected and provided. Though the world has encountered the Lord Yeshua in flesh, there is still the need to reveal what that flesh really was as the Word incarnate. In Genesis 3 Yeshua was prophetically defined as the Word to become flesh, or the covering for humanity. Yeshua is the Word made flesh; He is the tabernacle for man. As the body of Yeshua, every person within Him is placed in who He is. Satan is constantly trying to be in the place of God. Satan attempts to be "god" by doing. He wants to position himself in the place of the Most High God. Satan is aware that God's position on earth is in His representative (Adam); therefore Satan attacks the image and likeness—man's identity.

The pieces of the armor Paul gave are the names of Yeshua as He appears throughout history. The church is fully clothed, armed and going into battle for a holy cause in Yeshua. Every kingdom established is challenged if not conquered. The kingdoms of this world rule by the god of this world, who constantly attempts to circumvent the rule and reign of God's sovereignty.

> For every [tramping] warrior's war boots and all his armor in the battle tumult and every garment rolled in blood shall be burned as fuel for the fire. For to us a Child is born, to us a Son is given; and the government shall be upon His shoulder, and His name shall be called Wonderful Counselor, Mighty God, Everlasting Father [of Eternity], Prince of Peace. Of the increase of His government and of peace there shall be no end, upon the throne of David and over his kingdom, to establish it and to uphold it with justice and with righteousness from the [latter] time forth,

even forevermore. The zeal of the Lord of hosts will perform this (Isaiah 9:5-7 AMP).

Yeshua's name is manifold in power and authority. As we go through each piece, I will explain each as a name referring to Yeshua. Within each piece of armor there is a nature that functions according to the nature designed in the name. But before I share the functions of the armor as it relates to Yeshua, it is necessary to understand the importance of names.

The Bible places a profound emphasis on the naming of every person, place or thing. Names meant everything to the people of the ancient biblical world; the reputation or name is something for which to live or die. An example of naming can be seen in the twelve sons of Israel; they all were named based on what took place and who they were meant to become (see Genesis 29–30). In Hebrew the name of a person is related to the person's character and in many cases is the recognition of whom they worship.

Names often indicated a relationship between the person and the one who gives the name (see Genesis 35:18; 2 Samuel 12:24). Names also denoted character (see 1 Samuel 25:25) and a person's purpose, as seen in Moses. To dishonor a name was to dishonor a person as in forgetting (see Jeremiah 23:27). To be baptized in the name of someone was to transfer ownership (see Matthew 28:19; 1 Corinthians 1:13, 15). And to rightfully use a name of another was to use that person's authority.

The name of Yeshua is all-conquering. It is the name that is above every other name in heaven and on earth. It is in this name that every knee shall bow and every tongue confess His Lordship as King, of things in heaven and things in earth and things in the underworld. The armor of the Lord is Yeshua Himself, and believers are truly hidden in Him. The identity we have is through our adoption, whereby we take on His name or authority, character and reputation.

I will use the same order Paul does. In each piece there is "spiritual" DNA as indicated by the Hebrew letters. To reveal the person of Yeshua, each name will be broken down by the letters used to spell the name. The names of Yeshua all carry the character and nature of who He is. The spiritual significance in each piece of the armor will speak of Yeshua's absolute authority. This authority is the covering of nakedness whereby humanity is fully restored to the revelation of who we are as image and likeness of God. Salvation is wholeness and completion to and in God.

There are six pieces of armor; six is the number of man, and Adam was made on the sixth day as God's representative. The pieces are:

1. Belt of Truth—Emet
2. Breastplate of Righteousness—Tzedakah
3. Gospel of Peace—Shalom
4. Shield of Faith—Emunah
5. Helmet of Salvation—Yehoshua/Yeshua
6. Word of the Spirit, the Word of God—Ruach/Devar

# Chapter Six:

# Belt of Truth

"Stand firm therefore, having girded your loins with truth" (Ephesians 6:14).

## Emet

*Emet* (אמת) is the Hebrew word for truth. In the Hebrew alphabet emet is spelled, right to left, aleph-mem-tav. Emet comes from the verb *aman* meaning to support or make firm.

The letters used to spell emet are *aleph, mem* and *tav*. The first and last letters are the same ones used in the beginning of creation (את) and are all-encompassing. Truth begins, maintains and ends all of creation. Truth is the substance of God's intention and serves as the spiritual seal of God. This seal refers to the actual verification and realization of God's will in creation.

## Aleph

*Aleph* (א) is the first letter in emet and the first of the twenty-two letters in the Hebrew alphabet. It carries the numerical value of one. Aleph is the symbol of God's oneness and mastery. It is man in perfect unity with the infinite will of God.

The ancient Hebraic pictograph of aleph is that of an ox. The ox represents strength and power. Aleph alludes to the Hebrew word *aluph*, which means "master." Aleph is symbolized as the absolute unity of God; God is One. As the first letter it says there is none other besides Him: one, single and unique.

Aleph makes no sound, in allusion to the hidden mysteries of God. There are two letters hidden in aleph (א). They are a slanted vav (ו) and two yuds (י); each has the numerical value of ten, thereby equaling twenty. The two letters within aleph combined carry the value of twenty-six ($6 + 10 + 10 = 26$), the same numerical value of the unpronounced name of God, YHVH [YUD (10) HEY (5) VAV (6) HEY (5)]. Truth begins as God and ends as God.

## Mem

*Mem* (מ) is the thirteenth letter of the Hebrew alphabet and the second letter in the word *emet*. Mem has a numerical value of forty. It is the symbol of the revealed and the concealed Moses/Messiah. Moses represents the written word of Torah. The Messiah, Yeshua, represents the fulfillment of God's Word. Mem speaks of the openly revealed glory of God in action. It also is the concealed mysteries of God's omnipresence. God remains unknowable, invisible, indivisible and hidden. The depth of His being is beyond intellect; yet He reveals as He chooses to.

Mem, in ancient Hebrew pictography, is symbolized as water. Water in Hebrew is *mayim* and represents the mighty and blood. The water of man is considered to be the blood because it flows throughout the body. To the ancient Hebrews water was a mystery and often was identified with God.

## Tav

The final letter of emet is *tav* (ת). Tav is the twenty-second letter, the last of the Hebrew alphabet. Tav has a numerical value of four hundred. As the last letter it represents perfection and truth. This perfection is the eternal intention of God in the original state prior to man's fall in the garden. Tav is a letter of stability; it is man's final destination. In other words, truth is the place of God's judicial pronouncement. Judicial pronouncement is the rule and reign in the realm of God. Tav is the "kingdom of the infinite One." Tav is faithfulness in the power of completion of divine service.

The pictographic symbol for tav is two crossed sticks forming either a cross or an X. It represents a seal in covenant. In this case X does mark the spot. As a final letter in the alphabet, emet, and the all-encompassing first and last, tav speaks of being the final expression of God and His Word.

> Jesus said to him, "I am the way, and the truth, and the life; no one comes to the Father but through Me" (John 14:6).

Yeshua is the Truth in John. He is the "I AM." Luke 22:70 says, "And they all said, 'Are You the Son of God, then?' And He said to them, 'Yes, I am.'" Seeing him as the I AM, men fell back, because the Truth demands worship by obedience. Whether those men wanted to or not, they fell because of the nature of Truth.

The belt to a soldier was a very important piece of the armor—everything he valued went into the belt. What is most important to Yeshua is His Father's will. A belt around the waist is to gird or bind the offspring to the Lord. The loins represent seed, which represent a continuance. Yeshua's position establishes the will of God which is for man to rule over creation. By the obedience of Yeshua he becomes the first and last word on this rulership in which everything is subject to Him.

As the way, the truth and the life Yeshua reveals emet as the substance of His own name. As aleph and tav (alpha and omega) He declares the beginning and end. Mem as the middle letter is truly the first letter to restoring order. This illustration reveals Yeshua as the Anointed One, King of kings, Lord of lords, ruling and reigning as Truth.

22  21 20 19  18  17 16 15 14 13 12 11 10 9  8  7  6  5  4  3  2  1

א ב ג ד ה ו ז ח ט י כ ל מ נ ס ע פ צ ק ר ש ת

400 300  200 100  90 80  70  60 50 40  30  20 10

The top row corresponds with the sequential order, and the bottom row indicates the numerical value of each letter. The letter towering above all is lamed (ל), the twelfth one. Lamed's numerical value is thirty. There are eleven letters before lamed and ten letters after it. As the tallest letter, it also represents Yeshua as the King. The letter *mem*, being the first letter after lamed and the center letter in emet, brings and begins the order of God. Eleven denotes lawlessness, transition, divine rule decreased, disorder, incompleteness, disorganization and disintegration.[4]

Lamed is the twelfth letter, and it represents foundation, governmental perfection, tribes, apostles and prophets. Twelve represents kingdom order in sovereignty and worship. Lamed represents the kingship of Yeshua that establishes order. The number ten is designated to present law and order, commandment, ownership, restoration, covenant and the double manifestation of divine grace.

The numerical value of lamed is thirty. It alludes to the priesthood and how Yeshua brought forth the kingdom of God to fullness and order by establishing a body of people as truth in Him. Thirty is the age a priest would enter into service at the temple. It is believed that Yeshua began preaching repentance at the age of thirty, the age a Levite entered into priesthood service (see Numbers 4:2-49). Thirty is connected with redemption (see Exodus 21:32; Matthew 26:14-15; Zechariah 11:12-13).

Yeshua establishes the virtuous order for humanity to enter into God's sanctuary to find His love and refuge. When reading the letters in the alphabet from left to right (כלמ) using the final kaf, the word *melek* ("king") appears. Yeshua is King of kings because He is the Truth. He is not about truth, nor did He teach about truth. Truth is who He is.

Emet in its intellectual sense represents God's plan for reality, which follows His will and precedes His seal. Emet demands the experience of God. Man is granted the ability to experience God's power, and in doing so truth becomes the way of life. Emet is the power to realize one's own deepest potential, which is in fact the power of the soul to bring about the ultimate realization of God's potential.

Yeshua generates life to encounter truth. Truth is to live the will of God. Truth is obedience and faithfulness in motion. Truth is the character of a person and the restoration of the world in relation with God. God is the Ruach HaEmet, the Spirit of Truth (see John 14:17, 15:26, 16:13). This Spirit of Truth is the Ruach HaKodesh, the Holy Spirit. The Spirit of God's ministry is holiness, which brings His will into the earth realm in those that live in truth by the Spirit of Truth. David speaks of Yeshua as the truth in Psalm 25:4-5:

Make me know Your ways, O Lord; teach me Your paths. Lead me in Your truth and teach me, for You are the God of my salvation; for You I wait all the day.

God created Adam with the awareness of God as the Creator. Adam's awareness of God prior to sin gave him authority and power to rule creation. When Adam disobeyed the Word of God, truth was compromised, becoming only the knowledge of good and evil, which in turn produced lies. Truth was restored through Yeshua. Yeshua is authority and power. Yeshua rules as truth and eternal life. Truth is what seals us as believers in Yeshua. As believers in Yeshua, our greatest potential is truth because it is the ultimate comprehension of God's potential.

Finally all the trees said to the bramble, "You come, reign over us!" The bramble said to the trees, "If in truth you are anointing me as king over you, come and take refuge in my shade; but if not, may fire come out from the bramble and consume the cedars of Lebanon" (Judges 9:14-15).

# Chapter Seven:

# Breastplate of Righteousness

"Having put on the breastplate of righteousness" (Ephesians 6:14).

*Tzedakah* is the Hebrew word for righteousness (צדקה). The letters *tzaddi, dalet, kof* and *hei* make up the word. Tzedakah gives the indication of straightness or rightness. This Old Testament word gives a sense of deliverance or salvation. During the time of Yeshua "righteousness" had come to mean helping the poor. Religious leaders had narrowed down Israel's worship of God to works of righteousness, including prayer and fasting. It was thought that the giving of alms was the most important act; this act of giving became synonymous with righteousness.

The Hebrew words *tzadik* ("righteous one") and *yashar* ("upright") are paralleled many times in the Bible, indicating that in the Hebrew mind they were similar in meaning. "Upright" is another abstract word, but it is often used in a concrete manner. In Jeremiah 31:9 it means "straight," as in a straight path.

The ancient Hebrews were a nomadic people who often traveled the same paths to pastures and campsites. Anyone who left these straight paths could become lost and wander in the wilderness.

A wicked person is seen as one lost on a crooked path, while a righteous person is one who remains on the straight path.

> Trust in the Lord with all your heart and do not lean on your own understanding. In all your ways acknowledge Him, and He will make your paths straight (Proverbs 3:5-6).

## Tzaddi

*Tzaddi* (צ) is the first letter in the word *tzedakah*. It is the eighteenth letter and denotes righteousness and humility. The letter *tzaddi* begins the word *tzelem*, the divine image in which God created man. Tzelem carries three conscious levels of soul: mind, heart and action, all of which are foundational to worship. The letter is viewed as a man in the posture of worship and signifies humility.

The ancient Hebrew pictographic image for the letter *tzaddi* is a fishhook, which represents catching, desire and need. Righteousness can be seen as the seeking of "rightness."

The Hebrew word for tree is *etz*; the tree was created on the third day of creation. The gematria for both tzelem (ם/40 ל/30 צ/90) and etz (צ/90 ע/70) is 160. We can relate this to Yeshua as the branch. Tzelem, when looking at the letter *tzaddi*, is the "divine image" in which man was created on the sixth day.

> In that day the branch of the Lord will be beautiful and glorious, and the fruit of the earth will be the pride and the adornment of the survivors of Israel (Isaiah 4:2).

Now listen, Joshua the high priest, you and your friends who are sitting in front of you—indeed they are men who are a symbol, for behold, I am going to bring in My Servant the Branch (Zechariah 3:8).

The letter *tzaddi*, sometimes shown as *tsade*, has the ancient Hebrew pictograph of lying on one's side, engaged in an ambush. The holy letter *tzaddi* is the ability to hunt in order to redeem and elevate. *Tsad* means side; the blood of redemption came from the side of Yeshua (see John 19:34).

**Dalet**
The second letter in tzedakah is *dalet* (ד). Dalet is the fourth letter of the Hebrew alphabet. It means "door." In the shape of the dalet can be seen a lintel and a post, like those of a door. Dalet symbolizes dimensions and concern. Dalet can also mean "pathway."

The door itself is the property of humility and lowliness. The dalet is also the initial letter of the word *dirah* ("dwelling place"), as in the phrase, "[God's] dwelling place below." Thus the full meaning of the dalet is the door through which the humble enter into the realization of God's dwelling place below.

So Jesus said to them again, "Truly, truly, I say to you, I am the door of the sheep" (John 10:7).

For the Lord will pass through to smite the Egyptians; and when He sees the blood on the lintel and on the two doorposts, the Lord will pass over the door and will not allow the destroyer to come in to your houses to smite you (Exodus 12:23).

Righteousness is the door for every person who accepts Yeshua as the way to God. It is in Yeshua we have access to the Creator of all things, as can be seen when Yeshua speaks of being the way in John 14:6.

Dalet is connected to both the upper world (heaven) and the lower world (earth). The lintel reaches across, representing God in His eternal kingdom; the side post, which represents man in uprightness, is connected to that kingdom. Yeshua serves to mediate between God and man through redemption and reconciliation.

> For there is one God, and one mediator also between God and men, the man Christ Jesus, who gave Himself as a ransom for all, the testimony given at the proper time (1 Timothy 2:5-6).

## Kuf/Kof

*Kuf* (ק) is the third letter in tzedakah and is the nineteenth letter of the Hebrew alphabet. Kuf, sometimes seen as *kof*, symbolizes holiness and growth. It consists of two letters, *kaf* (כ) (20) and *vav* (ו) (6) = 26. This is the same gematria for the sacred name of the Lord: YUD (10) HEY (5) VAV (6) HEY (5). The sacred name of God connects kuf to holiness, which conveys the supremacy of God. Kuf has a numerical value of one hundred or ten times ten. This speaks of increased responsibility and covenant possession.

Kuf is the first letter for the Hebrew word for sacrifice, *korban*. It is rooted in the word *close*. Korban literally means that which has been brought close and refers to the sacrifice of something that enters into God's presence in the sanctuary.

The ancient Hebrew pictograph for kuf is represented by an image of a horizon. The horizon is the place where light gathers. This light is seen as a revolution or circle. Kuf is attached to the cycles or the return to the point of origin.

In You, O Lord, I have taken refuge; let me never be ashamed. In Your righteousness deliver me and rescue me; incline Your ear to me and save me. Be to me a rock of habitation to which I may continually come; You have given commandment to save me, for You are my rock and my fortress (Psalm 71:1-3).

## Hei

*Hei* (ה) is the final letter of tzedakah. Hei is the fifth letter of the Hebrew alphabet and carries the same numerical value. It is the breath letter; when spoken, it requires very little effort and is pronounced "hey." Hei is also the divinity letter. As the fifth letter it represents grace. The letter shape has an opening shown to the left and is seen as the place whereby God allows all who are willing to enter into His protection and provision.

The ancient Hebrew pictograph of this letter is an image of a person with hands extended upward toward the heavens, which alludes to the acceptance into God's beloved. Hei is the letter connected to God's life and power. This connection through God's breath is His mercy and grace whereby repentance unites everyone who believes salvation is in righteousness.

Traditionally righteousness in Christian doctrine is the righteousness of Yeshua and what He accomplished. Righteousness is a descriptive name for Yeshua; it is seen as a gift of God given at the moment of the acceptance in Yeshua, which enables the process of sanctification to take place and leads to holiness. In a wider sense righteousness carries meanings of uprightness, virtue, innocence, faultlessness, guiltlessness and approval from God.

In His days Judah will be saved, and Israel will dwell securely; and this is His name by which He will be called, the Lord our righteousness (Jeremiah 23:6).

Righteousness is the fulfillment of a claim. God's claim on redemption is His divine authority over all that belongs to Him. God's correction places us in correct moral posture; it will cause us to stand in opposition to a lie. In correction there is the manifestation of the unchanging truth, both inwardly and outwardly. During the course of correction there will be discipline. Discipline is ongoing in uprightness, whereby as sons and daughters loved by God believers are able to stand erect and confirm His abounding love.

Righteousness involves two dimensions, the first being moral integrity, loyalty and rightness. The second aspect of righteousness is straightness, like a straight pathway. Hosea 14:9 says, "The ways of the Lord are right, and the righteous [morally straight] will walk in them." Righteousness is the perfect standard of God's nature. The moral character of God is expressed in righteousness because He is righteous and all He does is righteous.

God is not governed by any standard or law external to Himself; according to His own consistent and pure standard, God is the full measure of His holiness, His distinction and the pure essence of His plan. Righteousness makes the believer accountable to God just as Yeshua was. Yeshua is the righteous one. And as the righteous one His obedience is the light in which believers in Him walk.

The breastplate for a soldier was light to provide ease of movement as it protected the wearer. The breastplate was attached to the belt and protected the heart, which is *lev* in Hebrew. Lev symbolizes inside authority. This authority is in and through Yeshua as the upright. It is in Yeshua that the believers come into the presence of God, as Adam was in the beginning; it is a place that is set aside for the purpose of bringing glory to the Father through obedience.

The steps of a man are established by the Lord, and He delights in his way (Psalm 37:23).

# Chapter Eight:

# Gospel of Peace

"And having shod your feet with the preparation of the gospel of peace" (Ephesians 6:15).

This part of the armor is the most important because shalom is foundational to reconciliation and restoration. The Hebrew word for peace is *shalom* (שלום). The root of shalom is *shalam*, a word used to express the idea of replacing or restoring. When we hear the word *peace*, we usually take it to mean an absence of war or strife; it doesn't mean this, however, in the ancient Hebrew. Shalam, a verb, literally means "to make whole and well" and implies "wholeness" of the person in health and prosperity. Shalam is usually used in the context of making restitution.

If one man's ox hurts another's so that it dies, then they shall sell the live ox and divide its price equally; and also they shall divide the dead ox. Or if it is known that the ox was previously in the habit of goring, yet its owner has not confined it, he shall surely pay ox for ox, and the dead animal shall become his (Exodus 21:35-36).

Shalom, or peace, is the foundation of the entire armor and is probably the most important aspect in understanding the name of Yeshua. Peace is covenantal language and serves as the glue in a real relationship with God. When the covenant was first enacted between God and Israel, some of the sacrifices were peace offerings, to celebrate the relationship between the people and God.

Shalom is the catalyst for salvation. In the meaning of shalom there is completeness, implying nothing missing and nothing broken. Shalom is the bridge to covenant. There is nothing missing because God sees the completeness of Adam reestablished. There is nothing broken because the covenant is restored between man and his Creator. Most sacrificial offerings were given entirely to God, but the peace (or fellowship) offering was different; the worshipper eats part of it, as if he is sharing a meal with God. This is the ultimate picture of friendship.

## Shin

The first letter in shalom is *shin* (ש). Shin is the twenty-first letter and has a numerical value of three hundred. It symbolizes divine power and script and appears to have three heads across the top. These represent the soul, *nefesh*; the body, *basar*; and the spirit, *ruach*. One of the meanings of the word *shin* in Hebrew is "change." In change there is the changeless essence of God. "For I, the Lord, do not change" (Malachi 3:6). This is the paradoxical latent presence of the power of change within the changeless, the "immovable power" that causes all motion.

One of the Hebrew names for God is El Shaddai, or Almighty God. Shaddai is paramount to divine power. Within the name Shaddai is the word *dai*, which means "enough." Dai reveals enough from the One who is the unlimited. The connection of dai to shin is in creation. There are laws within the nature of creation in which the infinite presence of divine power exists. In the course of God's calling forth creation, He also says "enough." Had He not done so, creation would have kept creating. Shin is the source where God revealed Himself as El Shaddai to show His power as master of the universe.

Shin also represents God's army, connecting it to the manifestation of His divine power. Shin's numerical value of three hundred correlates to a faithful remnant. The Bible records three hundred cubits as the size of the ark that kept Noah and his family safe; they were the first remnant (see Genesis 6:13-15, 7:21-23). The next remnant connected to the number three hundred is Gideon's chosen men of valor who went into battle on behalf of Israel (see Judges 7). A final example is the three hundred shields of beaten gold, each weighing three pounds, that Solomon makes (see 1 Kings 10:17). All these point to the faithful remnant of God's army in the body of Yeshua.

The ancient Hebrew pictograph for shin is the image of teeth, which represent chewing. This chewing alludes to overcoming the enemy, as Yeshua has.

> I will not be afraid of ten thousands of people who have set themselves against me round about. Arise, O Lord; save me, O my God! For You have smitten all my enemies on the cheek; You have shattered the teeth of the wicked. Salvation belongs to the Lord; Your blessing be upon Your people! Selah (Psalm 3:6-8).

## Lamed

The second letter in shalom is the twelfth letter, *lamed* (ל). It has a numerical value of thirty. Lamed has been discussed previously, but there are insights here that are relevant to the word *shalom*.

Lamed symbolizes teaching and purpose. The literal meaning of lamed is "to learn." In Jewish thought to learn is to teach, and to teach is to learn. Throughout the narrative record of the life of Yeshua we see that He taught the disciples constantly. Worship without study was and is a foreign concept to a Jew. Study is to work. This work brings a person to a place of perceiving a holy and great God.

The ancient Hebrew pictograph of lamed is a shepherd's staff. As the letter associated with teaching, lamed correlates to a shepherd's staff because it is used to guide and correct livestock, particularly sheep or goats. In addition, a shepherd's staff was also used as a weapon to defend and protect sheep from predators. The main purpose of a shepherd's staff was to move the animal in the intended direction.

In a biblical context a staff is symbolic of authority and bringing the will of a person under subjection. As the twelfth letter, lamed represents the establishment of God's kingdom and the executing of His will and authority. Yeshua has all power and authority, and His Lordship brings all things under subjection.

## Vav

The third letter of the word *shalom* is *vav* (ו). The numerical value of vav is six, and it symbolizes completion, redemption and transformation. Vav is sometimes referred to as *vav hachibur,* the "vav of connection" or "and."

The first vav in the Word of God is seen in Genesis: "In the beginning God created the heavens and [vav] the earth." It serves to join spirit and matter, heaven and earth, throughout creation. This vav appears at the beginning of the sixth word of Genesis and is the twenty-second letter of the verse. It alludes to the power to connect and inter-relate all twenty-two letters of the Hebrew alphabet, from aleph to tav.

The word *et*, which appears before the two instances of the word *the* in the above verse, is spelled aleph-tav and is generally taken to represent all the letters of the alphabet, from aleph to tav. Rabbis interpret the word in this verse to include all the various objects of creation present within heaven and earth.

Vav's pictograph is a peg or nail and shows securing or adding two things together. In the letter *vav* all parts of creation are secured in place according to their nature. When the nature of creation functions by divine design, life is retained.

## Mem

The last Hebrew letter in the word *shalom* is the final *mem* (ם). A final letter is called a *sofit*, and there are five in the Hebrew alphabet. A sofit appears differently but maintains the same pronunciation. Originally a sofit was used to indicate the end of a sentence or pause in reading. Mem is one of those letters.

This final letter is key to the word *peace*. Mem, the thirteenth letter, has a numerical value of six hundred. Mem's numerical value is symbolically important. Six hundred represents blessing and the manifold greatness of God's blessing. Genesis 7:11 speaks of the flood occurring in the six hundredth year of Noah's life. Solomon built the Holy of Holies using six hundred talents of gold. Mem is significant in revealing how Yeshua is manifold blessings from heaven. Yeshua as the *Sar Shalom* (Prince of Peace) has entered into the Holy of Holies, reconciling man and God (see Isaiah 9:6).

> Be anxious for nothing, but in everything by prayer and supplication with thanksgiving let your requests be made known to God. And the peace of God, which surpasses all comprehension, will guard your hearts and your minds in Christ Jesus (Philippians 4:6-7).

Shalom is critical to salvation. The gospel of peace is imperative to the person of Yeshua. Peace is thought by many to refer to times without war or conflict, but in this context peace would not fully express who we are as believers in Yeshua. Shalom implies a deeper spiritual significance from the standard meaning we are used to.

In the Garden of Eden, shalom was a mode of travel. Adam walked with the Lord because he was whole and complete prior to sin; his feet were shod with peace. Why is peace placed on the feet? What does "shod" mean exactly? Shod is a term that means "wearing shoes"; it is commonly used in reference to horseshoes.

Originally, the term *rough shod* refers to horses shod with the nails projecting from the shoe in order to prevent slipping. There were several reasons for placing shoes on a horse. One was to correct motion; in pulling the horse, the shoes give them much more traction. Horses were also shoed to enlarge the size of their feet and in doing so enhance the horse's gait. (Despite this benefit, going barefoot is much healthier for a horse's foot.) How does all this relate to the feet being shod with peace? The foundation of salvation is supported by feet and peace. Salvation's simplest definition is deliverance through redemption.

> So Jesus said to them again, "Peace be with you; as the Father has sent Me, I also send you." And when He had said this, He breathed on them and said to them, "Receive the Holy Spirit" (John 20:21-22).

The first Adam walked with God; yet he was without feet as the human mind comprehends them to be. When Adam disobeyed the Lord he became aware of himself, but his perception prior to this was not carnal. Adam's comprehension was not through physical means but spiritual. When Adam's eyes were opened, it was comparative to a born-again occurrence only opposite to what believers experience.

When a person accepts Yeshua the eyes of the spirit-man are once again opened, and the person is returned to original perception. This is the born-again process for the believer; we see it in reverse in Adam.

When Adam walked with God, Adam traveled at the speed of light, this light being the revelation of seeing God. Light makes seeing possible. The covering upon the feet is flesh which symbolically hides original relationship between man and God. This covering is a type of brokenness. Prior to the separation, Adam existed as God's agent in the spirit realm. Adam had no need of shoes because he walked in and with the glory of the Lord.

The connection to feet is in the restoration of a born-again experience. Adam once walked with God and was able to perceive God as completion, restitution and wholeness; this is peace. Feet are usually connected to shoes; shoes enclose feet. In a biblical context shoes represent enclosure of man's spirit. Shoes are garments that symbolize a person's staying connected to the earth realm. Shoes serve as a garment just as the body serves as a garment for the soul. Shoes serve as a typology symbolizing the enclosure of man's soul as attached to the natural sphere.

Throughout the Bible there are countless references to feet and shoes. They are a significant part of insight into the relationship between man and God. I encourage you to read the following passages to learn more: Genesis 49:9-11; Exodus 3: 4-6; Deuteronomy 11:24-25; Joshua 3:17-18; Joshua 5:14-15; Ruth 3:3-5; Psalm 18:32-34; Psalm 56:12-13; Isaiah 41:1-3; Luke 8:34-36; Luke 15:21-23; John 12:3; John 13:5-10; Matthew 28:8-9; and Acts 3:6-8.

In the context of armor shalom is about restitution of mankind to the Creator. It is complete wholeness. When Adam's eyes were opened the spirit-man died, fragmenting them (male and female) and making them spiritual blind. When his spiritual eyes were open, time as we know it did not exist for Adam. There was not a confinement to the body. Sin made us captive to time; man became aware of a beginning and an ending. As eternal beings in the image and likeness of God, we were never meant to have an ending. How can someone made in the image and likeness of an eternal, self-sufficient One have such an understanding of time? As Adam walked with the Lord, he also was able to transcend all those things that would limit his relationship with his Creator. Sin made us captive to ourselves and therefore outside of eternity.

*Shabah* (שבה) is the Hebrew word for captive. In ancient Hebrew the pictograph letters are *shin (*teeth representing pressing) and *bet* (representing tent). When placed together shin and bet gain a meaning of "pressing into the tent." This implies a turning back or away from someone or something; a captive is one turned away from a dwelling place. In the case of man sin brought Adam into an awareness, and his flesh became his dwelling place instead of the Lord. Shabah denotes a returning to one's place of residence or where one sits.

In redemption, salvation (Yeshua) takes captivity captive by returning humanity to their original dwelling place, the Creator. The numerical value of shin is four hundred and bet is two bringing a total of 402. Reduced to its smallest value, 402 becomes six (4 + 0 + 2 = 6), the number of man or Adam.

> The Spirit of the Lord is upon me, because he hath anointed me to preach the gospel to the poor; he hath sent me to heal the brokenhearted, to preach deliverance to the captives, and recovering of sight to the blind, to set at liberty them that are bruised, to preach the acceptable year of the Lord (Luke 4:18-19 KJV).

As long as there is salvation in the world, it is a matter of choice when people refuse to be captive to God. Sinful nature is bondage by choice, the choice made in the garden. In a "logistical" way there is no captivity outside of God because all is His (see Deuteronomy 10:13-15).

God's Word became flesh, lived, died and was resurrected and is now alive in God with God. God's love made His Word available again. Sin no longer holds any captive. It is the bondage of deception that still continues to keep humanity in the dark (see 2 Corinthians 3:16-4:7).

The gospel of peace is the Word of God speaking from heaven to earth, the message of wholeness, the returning to Him. When God speaks, He speaks beyond the mind and beyond the heart to the feet. Yeshua as Sar Shalom, the Prince of Peace, covers believers through immersion into His name. Reconciliation is the message of His name. The Hebrew word for name is *shem*, which consists of the letters *shin* and *mem*. This forms the root for *neshamah*, the Hebrew word for soul. This expresses that the substance of one's soul is the name. The essence of a name is pivotal to peace. A name represents the character of a person or place and also confers authority. The covenant that is renewed through Yeshua serves as a shoe, clothing the soul so we may once again see and walk with the Creator.

The final and most definitive aspect of feet is seen on the cross, where the feet of Yeshua were nailed. On the cross Yeshua makes a definitive statement that opens man to his eternal destiny: "It is finished." Then He breathes His last breath. Salvation (Yeshua) is being conveyed as is the last word in the conversation of sin and death. The law of sin which resulted in the separation of man from his Creator is dealt the final blow. In short, "Satan, there is nothing more to discuss or debate on this issue. I AM! the last word on the subject of sin."

The word used for "finished" in John 19:30 is the Greek *teleo*. It is the reconnection or the completed continuation of the unbreakable Word of God. When Yeshua breathes His last breath the spirit returns the original destiny of man's soul to be "living" as designed by the Creator Himself. "It is finished" (see John 19:29-31) is a definitive point of returning to the Divine with full identity of authority.

The Word of God is eternal, and the perimeters of God's kingdom are absolute. It is not by works that anyone is saved, and the ultimate example of reconciliation is Yeshua.

The feet are freed from bondage through the covering of shalom. There is no more nakedness because we are covered in the righteousness of Yeshua. Until salvation is heard and received, revelation from God cannot be seen because of the shame of nakedness. It sounds backward; but in our nakedness we are covered, and in Yeshua's covering we are naked. To put it another way man attempts to cover up, and Yeshua uncovers, thereby bringing us to dwell with God. The gift of God is life again.

The preparation of feet with the gospel of peace is very critical to experiencing the fullness of who we are in and through the Mashiach, the Anointed One. Because of this, Satan tries to speak to the feet (our walk) where he attempts to make us subject to him. All things have been placed underfoot; therefore the feet are critical to shalom. Satan's plan consists of maintaining brokenness in our relationship with the Lord. He uses strategies that attempt to nullify the covenant Yeshua established through His feet on the cross.

Then Peter said unto her, How is it that ye have agreed together to tempt the Spirit of the Lord? Behold, the feet of them which have buried thy husband are at the door, and shall carry thee out. Then fell she down straightway at his feet, and yielded up the ghost: and the young men came in, and found her dead, and, carrying her forth, buried her by her husband (Acts 5:9-10 KJV).

Every believer is set apart to bring kingdom peace. Shalom upon the feet is the correction of God Himself; by His Word He restores the order of the spirit within man. Nothing is missing in salvation, the Prince of Peace, and the covenant is placed back in God through Yeshua. Believers in Yeshua are no longer naked in sin.

Therefore humble yourselves [demote or lower yourselves in your own estimation] under the mighty hand of God, that in due time He may exalt you, casting the whole of your care [all your anxieties, all your worries, all your concerns, once and for all] on Him, for He cares for you affectionately and cares about you watchfully. Be well balanced [temperate, sober of mind], be vigilant and cautious at all times; for that enemy of yours, the devil, roams around like a lion roaring in fierce hunger, seeking someone to seize upon and devour (1 Peter 5:6-8 AMP).

Shoes, while not traditional pieces of armor, kept a soldier from feeling the bare ground. Sandals were commonly worn and provided very little protection; they could hardly be used as a weapon in battle. Peace is upon the feet to restore what was missing—the relationship man was destined to have with God—and what was broken, the word that spoke who we were by the revelation of God.

Therefore My people shall know My name; therefore in that day I am the one who is speaking, 'Here

I am.'" How lovely on the mountains Are the feet of him who brings good news, Who announces peace And brings good news of happiness, Who announces salvation, And says to Zion, "Your God reigns!" (Isaiah 52:6-7).

# Chapter Nine:

# Shield of Faith

"In addition to all, taking up the shield of faith with which you will be able to extinguish all the flaming arrows of the evil one" (Ephesians 6:16).

The Hebrew word for faith is *emunah* (אמונה). Emunah is being active in support. This is important because the Western concept of faith places the action on the one in which faith is placed, such as having "faith in God" or "trusting in Him." The Hebrew view of faith is remaining in a place by being faithful or loyal. It places the action on the one who places faith in God. Faith is not knowing God will act, but being willing to do what one can to support God and His acts through obedience and allegiance. This Hebraic view of faith can be seen in Exodus 17:12 when Israel battles the Amalekites as Moses lifts his hands upward.

But Moses' hands grew weary; so they took a stone and put it under him, and he sat upon it, and Aaron and Hur held up his hands, one on one side, and the other on the other side; so his hands were steady [emunah] until the going down of the sun.

Aaron and Hur provided the support as they held Moses' arms, not by Moses himself. When we say, "I have faith in God," we should be thinking, "I will do what is required to support God." What we say when we mimic the position of Moses in Exodus 17 is that we are willing to stay where God commands regardless of the cost. Faithfulness is to understand God's will. Again Eema gives another great definition for understanding; she defines it as to "stand under." Clarified it is getting under the thing you comprehend and upholding it with all your might. Whatever a person believes to be truth should be upheld with everything that is within the person; this is what faith is all about.

The word *steady* in Exodus 17 is the Hebrew word *emunah*. It denotes faithfulness and fidelity. Faith is always related to being loyal, as a man and woman are in marital covenant. When a man and a woman are married they enter into covenant. By original design the first thing that must be in place is loyalty to God from the two of them as individuals. Then they agree to support this faithfulness with each other.

Hababbuk 2:4 says the "just shall live by his faith." This is often translated as "trust" or "belief," but this is not the case; it should be interpreted as "the righteous live by his faithfulness." Justice is always devoted and committed to what is right. In the book of Hebrews, chapter 11 is foundational for most Christian believers. The passage is written later in the historical account of faithful community of Hebrew believers. The concept of "trust" and "belief" as defined and used today would have been foreign to the first believers (see James 2:18-26). Instead of reading this chapter with the word *faith*, I encourage people to read this chapter by replacing "faith" with "faithfulness." Those mentioned in Hebrews 11 are people who were faithful. The shield of faith is only effective when fidelity remains in place.

## Aleph

*Aleph* (א) is the first letter in the word *emunah*. As mentioned previously, aleph is the first letter of the Hebrew aleph-bet and has a numerical value of one represented to mean master. As the master letter, strength and leadership are through faithfulness. Aleph in the word *emunah* illustrates a spiritual principle: the Lord is constantly faithful even when He goes unseen.

The first thing in God is His love because He is love. It is not an emotion that He gives; it is His attribute of justice and kindness. Man is the only part of creation whereby God's love is His faithfulness. As the first letter, aleph is the source of all beginnings and serves as the throne of God's sovereignty. Every believer in Yeshua establishes God's kingdom through their faithfulness, and this is the origin of complete obedience.

"Faithful is He who calls you, and He also will bring it to pass" (1 Thessalonians 5:24).

## Mem

*Mem* (מ) is the next letter in the word *emunah* and is the thirteenth letter of the Hebrew alphabet. It has a numerical value of forty. Mem signifies the revealed and the concealed. God's concealment does not bring distance but closeness. God's revelation does not bring knowledge but relationship. The sages have said the shape of the letter denotes humility; it reminds us to bend ourselves in God's presence.

The pictographic of mem is water. Water in ancient times was seen as the "unknown" as in relating to "whom"? In the days of Noah when the flood occurred, rain was an unknown event. The waters covered the earth, and man encountered the power of the Creator. The deluge of forty days and nights shows God's grace in new beginnings. When looking at the letter *mem*, there is a bowing, expressing obedience. The flood represents the cleansing and return of creation to fruit-fulness, multiplicity and having dominion by subduing.

Mem is symbolically kingship and dominion through revival and renewal. In kingship there is mutual faithfulness. The nature of faithfulness instinctively submits knowing it is God's distinct nature.

> Know therefore that the Lord your God, He is God, the faithful God, who keeps His covenant and His loving-kindness to a thousandth generation with those who love Him and keep His commandments (Deuteronomy 7:9).

**Vav**

*Vav* (ו) is the next letter in the word *emunah*. It is the sixth letter of the alphabet and has a numerical value of six. Vav consists of a single vertical line. This line is a connector and serves as the mediator between Hebrew words and phrases.

Man was created as the image and likeness on the sixth day (see Genesis 1:26-31), and as the sixth letter, vav represents the relationship between the divine and human nature because of the image and likeness of Adam. Vav plays a significant grammatical role in emunah; when it is prefixed to a verb in Scripture it changes the tense from past to future, or vice versa. This implies the timelessness of the letter *vav*; true faith is untouched by history. Man is only as faithful as his ability to perceive eternal things. Adam's walk was without sin or death prior to his walking away and therefore was without time as we experience time and consequently "ageless"; this state of being operates as the connection between Adam and God.

Emunah is the essential connection or covenant between Israel and God. It is the essential key to the faithfulness of Yeshua for all who enter into covenant. His faithfulness is absolute. Faith is not trust or belief, though these are related to faith. Trust deals with the recognition of total dependency on God. This is an important interaction in the Hebrew mind. God was never concerned with Israel's trust and belief in Him; He was more concerned with their allegiance to their covenant with Him. The true function of a soul is to sustain and reinforce the consciousness of God's faithfulness through the Word of God.

> I will sing of the lovingkindness of the Lord forever; to all generations I will make known Your faithfulness with my mouth. For I have said, lovingkindness will be built up forever; in the heavens You will establish Your faithfulness. I have made a covenant with My chosen; I have sworn to David My servant (Psalm 89:1-3).

## Nun

*Nun* (נ) is the next letter of the Hebrew alphabet and has a numerical value of fifty. Nun symbolizes faithfulness, the soul and its manifestation. Its ancient Hebrew pictographic image is a seed sprout, which denotes continuation and life. Nun is the manifestation of offspring, which perpetuates a kingdom. Nun always points to heirs, inheritance and heritage. Nun, as a generational letter, expresses faithfulness as everlasting.

Within the letter *nun* is hidden the sixth Hebrew letter *vav*, (ו) representing man. Nun is the bending letter alluding to man being bent before the eternal Father. Man before God is in a servant's posture. The rabbis believe there are two ways in serving God: through the faithfulness and the congregation of humble people. In serving God in these ways, God elevates the person in Him. This servant aspect of nun represents man's ability to attain an elevated place in God through the bending of the mind, will and emotion in submission before Him.

Therefore humble yourselves under the mighty hand of God, that He may exalt you at the proper time (1 Peter 5:6).

Adam's attempt to be like God in Genesis 3 initiated his separation from God. This disconnect resulted in sin nature becoming the covering and removed man's ability to serve God. Sin in Hebrew is *chattat*, which means "to miss the mark." Sin in Hebraic thinking is the failure to fulfill something in God. A sinner is a person who has missed his or her potential and purpose in God.

Nun connects faithfulness to man's divine destiny, a destiny to serve the Lord in spirit and in truth. Mankind throughout every generation is destined to serve God as part of His creation. It is through the faithfulness of Yeshua that every believer continues to stand in the unwavering faith as an upright and trustworthy servant.

For the Lord is good; His lovingkindness is everlasting; and His faithfulness to all generations (Psalm 100:5).

## Hei

*Hei* (ה) is the last letter of the word *emunah*. It is the fifth letter of the alphabet and has a numerical value of five. Hei symbolizes divinity, gentility and specificity. Its pictographic image represents beholding and revelation. It is the sigh a person exhales upon revelation of a great sight. God revealed Himself to Abraham, Isaac and Jacob. He later revealed Himself to Israel on Mt. Sinai. In doing this He says, "Behold."

Trust in the Lord forever, for in God the Lord, we have an everlasting Rock (Isaiah 26:4).

There is little movement of lip, tongue and mouth when pronouncing hei. This suggests the effortlessness by God during the creation of the world. There is truly nothing too difficult for God.

> By the word of the Lord the heavens were made, and by the breath of His mouth all their host (Psalm 33:6).

Hei is commonly used as a prefix to words to mean "the," as in *ha'arets*, which means "the land." Adam was created from dust (land) and carries the breath of God.

> Then the Lord God formed man of dust from the ground, and breathed into his nostrils the breath of life; and man became a living being (Genesis 2:7).

Hei as the fifth letter is considered the letter of grace. The breath of God is His faithfulness dwelling within man.

> The Spirit of God has made me, and the breath of the Almighty gives me life (Job 33:4).

The word *emunah* is rooted in the word *aman*, which means "support." Emunah carries a meaning of building up or supporting. In Jewish thought belief in God is like a craft, a skill, or set of techniques that is studied and perfected over time. It is not something one is either born with or not.

Israel is referred to as a kingdom of priests called out to serve God. The history of Israel demonstrates its loyalty to God through faithfulness to the covenant. When Israel obeyed the commandments God responded in His faithfulness. The steadfastness of the community of Israel promised God's protection and provision.

"Now then, if you will indeed obey My voice and keep My covenant, then you shall be My own possession among all the peoples, for all the earth is Mine; and you shall be to Me a kingdom of priests and a holy nation." These are the words that you shall speak to the sons of Israel (Exodus 19:5-6).

Protection is essential to faith. A shield is not a weapon; the purpose of a shield is to defend and protect from harm. Yeshua is the faithful witness and the shield of God, just as God was faithful in shielding Israel. Believers' lives are hidden in Yeshua and therefore protected (see Colossians 3:2-4). Every believer serves as the continuation of the fullness of God's Word; therefore we are to exhibit that He is faithful.

And from Jesus Christ, the faithful witness, the firstborn of the dead, and the ruler of the kings of the earth to Him who loves us and released us from our sins by His blood—and He has made us to be a kingdom, priests to His God and Father—to Him be the glory and the dominion forever and ever. Amen (Revelation 1:5-6).

Yeshua is the faithful witness. As His kingdom prevails, His faithfulness is made known. Every believer's destiny is to return to what the Lord first instructed, which ultimately is faithfulness through obedience. Yeshua is the example of faithfulness. Salvation is not about "getting saved." Salvation in the greater sense is "becoming faithful." It's not saying "I'm saved" but "I'm faithful."

The disciples of Yeshua followed Him in word and deed. The community of believers did not think of themselves as "saved" or that they "got saved" in the modern Christian sense. Faithfulness is unto the Lord through covenant. It is beyond the realm of "Christianity" as many define it to be. The shield of faith is God's testimony to the believer. As believers the position of response is being a witness to God's faithfulness. The acceptance of God's grace is the acceptance of being faithful. Daily transformation is who we are to God, to ourselves in Yeshua and to those around us through conviction and devotion.

For I proclaim the name of the Lord; ascribe greatness to our God! The Rock! His work is perfect, for all His ways are just; a God of faithfulness and without injustice, righteous and upright is He (Deuteronomy 32:3-4).

# Chapter Ten:

# Helmet of Salvation

"And take the helmet of salvation" (Ephesians 6:17).

The Hebrew word for salvation is *Yeshua* (ישוע), also seen as *Yehoshua*. The name Yehoshua means "the Lord saves" and comes from the Hebrew "to save." Salvation entails deliverance, victory, prosperity, health and welfare. *Yasha* is the primitive root of Yehoshua. Yasha means to be open, wide or free. Another root of Yehoshua is *yesha*, which is liberty, deliverance, prosperity, safety, salvation and saving.

Repentance is connected to salvation in the term *teshuvah*, the Hebrew word for repentance. Teshuvah is rooted in the concept of return, or *shivah*. The root of shivah is *shoov*, which means "to return." Returning to God is salvation, and this is repentance. Teshuvah is turning toward good. Adam turned away from his Creator in his disobedience. Disobedience to God was and remains the greatest betrayal of humanity. Evil/sin is an afterthought in the scope of Adam. Salvation is the means whereby humanity returns to the Divine. Repentance is literally "rescue." The active meaning in teshuvah is *shava*, a root which means "to be free." The name YHVH is present in Yehoshua, and YHVH is the Eternal.

## Yud

The first letter in Yehoshua is *yud* (י). Yud is the tenth letter of the Hebrew alphabet and has a numerical value of ten. It is in the shape of a simple point and is the smallest letter in the alphabet. Yud has the important job of being the first letter of the Tetragrammaton, YHVH (YUD-HEI-VAV-HEI). With its value of ten yud is considered the redemptive number. Israel was redeemed from Egyptian bondage after ten plagues. God rescues the small nation of Israel and brings it into covenant with Him. Yud is like Israel in its smallness.

The Lord did not set His love on you nor choose you because you were more in number than any of the peoples, for you were the fewest of all peoples (Deuteronomy 7:7).

Yud, as the smallest letter, reveals the humility of Israel, but God takes Israel into greatness as a holy people; this teaches us that greatness comes from humility. Moses is a wonderful example of this. Numbers 12:3 says, "Now the man Moses was very humble, more than any man who was on the face of the earth." Moses, as a divinely appointed agent, served as the deliverer of Israel from Egyptian bondage.

The ancient Hebrew pictograph of yud is an image that looks like an arm and hand. It represents work and the act of throwing. The Hebrew word for hand is *yad*, which also means power, might and authority.

The Lord begins salvation with His Spirit, which carries the might to accomplish His will. Zechariah 4:6 says, "'Not by might, nor by power, but by My Spirit,' says the Lord of Hosts." Here the Lord reveals Himself as YHVH Sabaoth, the Lord of hosts. It is the work of the Lord that brings salvation. In the letter *yud* the very least prevails and is able to confirm His covenant.

## Hei

The second letter in Yehoshua is *hei* (ה). It is the fifth letter and, as mentioned, represents divinity. Being a breath letter, hei is the life of the name Yeshua. It is an exhalation that brings about God's will. In this breath we see mercy and repentance. It is by the breath of God that the sinner is able to return to God. A wonderful example of this is in John 20:21-22, which says, "So Yeshua said to them again, 'Peace be with you; as the Father has sent Me, I also send you.' And when He had said this, He breathed on them and said to them, 'Receive the Holy Spirit.'" It is in this breathing upon the disciples that their spirits were once again revived. This gave them the ability to see the full revelation of God.

The feast day Shavuot (Pentecost) recorded in Acts 2 is not when the disciples were revived with the initial breath. What is known as Pentecost is the appointed time of Shavuot or the time God gave to celebrate the spring harvest. Jews believe it is the time God handed down the Torah on Mount Sinai (see Leviticus 23:15-21; Numbers 28:26; Deuteronomy 16:9-12). All males were required to be in Jerusalem for the Shavuot, or the Feast of Weeks (see Deuteronomy 16:16).

It is during Shavuot that the empowering came to carry the message of salvation. This feast marked the harvest and was to be celebrated in giving thanks to God for His provision. The outpouring of the Holy Spirit in Acts 2 is the recognition of the entire harvest for the souls in the kingdom of God.

The ancient Hebrew pictograph of the letter *hei* is a man with extended hands raised above his head. It embodies the idea of beholding. In the culture of the ancient Hebrews a breath was revelation. It carried the idea of revealing something or pointing something out. Hei corresponded to the revelation of God through beholding His breath. Look at this letter and see the opening on the left; it shows all are able to enter into Him freely by His grace. Yeshua came to give life and to give that life abundantly. The letter *hei* is the breath by which man lives.

## Vav

The next letter of salvation is the sixth Hebrew letter, *vav* (ו). It is the third letter in the name Yehoshua. Man's salvation is the center of God's purpose; He wants to restore man to the image and likeness of God. After the disobedience of Adam the control and manipulation of Satan began to rule humanity. The nature of transformation is the demonstration of completion through redemption.

Vav personifies continuity. In Hebrew the letter *vav* is a conjunction; it links words, sentences, paragraphs and phrases. It connects heaven to earth. The letter is shaped like a hook. In the Torah an absent vav signals the beginning of a chapter or the beginning of a new era or theme.

Vav is always a connection in action that unites man to God; it serves as a mediator. Vav unites in order to continue. God's intent is to continue the fullness of His Spirit. Yeshua is the mediator that serves to continue this fullness throughout God's kingdom in power and authority. This power and authority are the "landmark" that is to characterize heaven throughout time.

The pictograph of vav is a tent peg. These were used to prevent slippage of something; they secured something. Vav looks like a nail, and salvation secures us by nailing; Yeshua was nailed to the cross and did away with sin once and for all. He is the vav that secures humanity back to God.

## Shin

*Shin* is the next letter in Yehoshua. It is the twenty-first letter of the Hebrew alphabet and carries a numerical value of three hundred. Shin is characterized as divine power and corruption.

Shin appears to have three heads (ש), which alludes to the spirit, soul and body. It is the pure gratification of who we are as servants. Through learning and teaching we experience liberty as an ongoing experience and not an event at a church altar. The shin in salvation is the eternal bond between God and man.

The ancient Hebrew pictograph of shin appears as two front teeth to indicate chewing, as mentioned earlier. In Yeshua the consumption of the body during Pesach (Passover) is clearly demonstrated when identifying the lamb that takes away the sin of the world according to Yohannan the Immerser (John the Baptist).

When Yeshua entered into Jerusalem during the final days of His life, it is believed He arrived on the tenth day in the month of Aviv (Nisan). It was in this jubilant entry that the people identified Him as the Lord. They shouted, "Baruch haba bashem Adonai!" or, "Blessed is he who comes in the name of the Lord!" This moment is consummated when four days later these same people shouted, "Crucify Him!"

Exodus 12 explains how Israel was to identify a lamb that was without blemish on the tenth of Nisan and then four days later slaughter the selected lamb. The blood was a sign that identified houses during the night of Israel's exodus from Egypt; it showed that death could not enter in. Israel picked out its sacrificial lamb when Yeshua arrived in Jerusalem; the betrayal allowed Yeshua to finish His work. Neither Israel nor the Romans killed Yeshua, but they were both instruments in the hand of God used to bring about a greater manifestation of His glory.

The letter *shin* represents both righteousness and unrighteousness. Yeshua takes on the likeness of sin so the righteousness of God will be revealed. When we know we are accepted as His beloved, nothing can validate or nullify identity. In the armor of God shin signifies power and authority that overcome the world in order to come into that which was since the beginning.

You are from God, little children, and have overcome them; because greater is He who is in you than he who is in the world (1 John 4:4).

## Ayin

The last letter in the name of Yehoshua is *ayin* (ע). Ayin is the sixteenth letter and carries a numerical value of seventy. Ayin is representative of sight and insight and is a vital letter within the alphabet. Because it means "eye," it is known as the "eye letter" of the Hebrew aleph-bet. The eye brings the perception of the world into the human mind. Ayin, as the eye, is the window into the mind; it is the tool whereby we perceive natural things. Adam's eyes were opened to a natural understanding, but this limited his abilities in supernatural discernment.

Eyes biblically speaking are often represented to mean the whole person. Sight plays a significant and influential role. What is seen first will influence a person's mind. Sin was first perceived in an opening of eyes. Our outlook on life is directly connected to our eyes. They gauge how we present ourselves to others. Unfortunately believers can at times be more concerned with man's perspective than with God's. We want to be perceived correctly, as if we unconsciously manipulate people's perceptions of us in order to be acceptable. While doing this, we totally forfeit who God has destined us to be.

In Genesis 3, Satan approached Eve with a tactic that would cause the demise of mankind. It was her inability to see she was already like God that caused a misappropriation of man's designated position in God. The fall of Adam was the result of what was not seen, not what was seen. Since this fall people have been driven by what is seen, what appeals to the flesh.

What we see is often what we want to see. People go to great lengths to have what they want. People go into debt, make ill-intended promises and will even kill to gain a moment of satisfaction that all too quickly dissipates before the process repeats itself. Yeshua is the revelation of the Father. In John 15:9, Yeshua tells Philip, "He who has seen Me has seen the Father." Ayin is the letter whereby man comprehends the Word of God.

> I am the Light of the world; he who follows Me will not walk in the darkness, but will have the Light of life (John 8:12).

Yeshua is the revelation of His Father. Ayin is a letter that consummates salvation through God's revealing Word, His Son Yeshua. Ayin is the last letter in the Hebrew word *salvation* and acts as a *coup de grâce*, the final blow against darkness.

The pictograph for ayin is an eye, and it represents the window of knowledge. When Yeshua is made known to men, God is also made known; Yeshua is in the Father, and the Father is in Him. Yeshua is the light of the world and returns mankind to the Eternal One.

The Hebrew word for light is *owr*; it is the first utterance of God. This word consists of three letters: aleph (1) + vav (6) + reish (200). When broken down to its smallest form, owr has a numerical value of nine $(1 + 6 + 200 = 207 = 2 + 0 + 7 = 9)$.

Thus the gematria of light is nine, the number signifying judgment. Salvation was ultimately wrought through the work of the cross when in the ninth hour Yeshua cries, "It is finished." This coupled with the three individual letters (aleph to represent the one true God as master of all; vav to represent man as Adam created on the sixth day; and reish to represent the glory of God) is seen in the 20 x 10. The number twenty in Scripture signifies the waiting for divine completion (see Genesis 21:38, 41; Judges 4:3; 1 Samuel 7:2).

The word *light*, spelled out using the ancient Hebrew pictograph, appears as the ox, a tent peg and the head of a man. The combination of these pictures expresses that the power of God has secured man as the head over all creation. Light is the ability to see God through Yeshua.

The Hebrew word for light means "enlighten" or "giver of light." The entire world perceived Yeshua on the cross, past, present and future, because salvation is completed in Him. Revelation is meant to bring relationship not knowledge. Yeshua's death is life crossing back over to God. In righteousness salvation is the judge of all things.

> Who shall give account to him that is ready to judge the quick and the dead? For this cause was the gospel preached also to them that are dead, that they might be judged according to men in the flesh, but live according to God in the spirit (1 Peter 4:4-6).

Judgment began and ended in two gardens, the first garden being the Gan Edin (Garden of Eden) and the last garden the Gat Shemanim (Gethsemane), which means "oil press." Salvation is the last man standing.

Ayin has the numerical value of seventy. Seventy symbolizes a season prior to increase. In Luke 10 seventy were sent out under the direction of Yeshua to bring about the kingdom of God through the working of signs and wonders. When the seventy returned to Him joyously, Yeshua told them not to be excited that demons were subject to them but that their name was written in the Book of Life. There is an increase in spiritual perception in the revelation of Yeshua.

Salvation is oneness with God in both His Word and will. Salvation cuts off and unites; it cuts off the self to unite a person to God. Salvation is more than believing in Yeshua. Salvation believes in God's Word, which is Yeshua. Yeshua was, is and will always be conceived as the word of God, the "I Am." The fullness of time brought forth the oneness of God's will. It was by sight that man fell. It is by sound that man is restored. "Let him who has ears to hear, hear." Hearing is the perception of the mind beyond the natural realm. The Word of the Lord is perceived through the eyes of the mind. Salvation restores the realization of God.

Salvation had to cover the mind, just as the helmet protects the head. With the mind of the Anointed One we are established as the body of Yeshua with him as the head of the body. He has overthrown all powers, breathed into us, secured us and broken the curse of sin.

In Yeshua ayin gives the concluding revelation as to who He is and who we are in Him. When Yeshua was praying for the disciples it was for all of them, including the believers of today and those to come. I will conclude this section with the words of Yeshua to the Father to remind us that we are sealed in Him who is salvation.

> For their sakes I sanctify Myself, that they them-
> selves also may be sanctified in truth. I do not ask on
> behalf of these alone, but for those also who believe
> in Me through their word; that they may all be one;
> even as You, Father, are in Me and I in You, that they
> also may be in Us, so that the world may believe that
> You sent Me. The glory which You have given Me
> I have given to them, that they may be one, just as
> We are one; I in them and You in Me, that they may
> be perfected in unity, so that the world may know
> that You sent Me, and loved them, even as You have
> loved Me. Father, I desire that they also, whom You
> have given Me, be with Me where I am, so that they
> may see My glory which You have given Me, for You
> loved Me before the foundation of the world. O righ-
> teous Father, although the world has not known You,
> yet I have known You; and these have known that

You sent Me; and I have made Your name known to them, and will make it known, so that the love with which You loved Me may be in them, and I in them (John 17:19-26).

# Chapter Eleven:

# Sword of the Spirit

"And the sword of the Spirit, which is the word of God" (Ephesians 6:17).

The word for spirit in Hebrew is *ruach* (רוח). The Ruach is the breath of God and the presence of God. This part of the armor is twofold, encompassing both the Spirit and Word. This unity of Spirit and Word is critical to the body of Yeshua, to all those who are born again. Ruach is often seen as divine inspiration.

> All Scripture is inspired by God and profitable for teaching, for reproof, for correction, for training in righteousness (2 Timothy 3:16).

The idea of the Ruach HaKodesh as inspiration is rabbinic in origin. The Ruach is the living manifested power of YHWH that leads, instructs, guides and teaches. The letters that make up the word *ruach* are reish, vav and chet. In Psalm 51:13 David refers to the "v'ruach kodsh'cho" (Your Holy Spirit) when beseeching God not to take the Spirit from him. The soul of all men seeks to fill the void of the Ruach. Some people attempt to fill their voids through various religious belief systems and others through fleshly fulfillment.

In the nostrils of man is the Ruach of God. The Ruach is the principle of life. It is the possession, the reason, the will which imparts life to man. The Ruach is life and imparts in order to establish and uphold life through guiding. The Ruach is the creative activity for the entire creation, from eternity to time and back to eternity. The best understanding is that the Ruach is the Author and Finisher of faithfulness.

> "The Spirit of God has made me, and the breath of the Almighty gives me life" (Job 33:4).

## Reish

*Reish* (ר) is the twentieth letter of the Hebrew alphabet and has a numerical value of two hundred. Reish signifies choice and is the mark of either distinction or deprivation. The pictograph of reish is the head of a man, which represents something that is the "head," "first" or "beginning." Reish represents the eternity of God as the only true living God because He is the head as Creator.

> In the beginning was the Word, and the Word was with God, and the Word was God. He was in the beginning with God. All things came into being through Him, and apart from Him nothing came into being that has come into being. In Him was life, and the life was the Light of men (John 1:1-4).

Yeshua is the Word that was in the beginning. The Word of God is the offspring of God; it comes out of Him. As this Word comes forth after the fall of man, it is always sent for redemptive purposes. The Word of God is the will of God, and it therefore executes His intentions. This is the role of Yeshua as the only begotten Son.

The shape of reish shows obedience as it bends to the dictates of God. Yeshua's example is the foremost example whereby every person who confesses His Lordship must then bow to the order of God's kingdom. Reish conveys the authority and power of Yeshua as the Word by the Spirit of God.

> And Jesus came up and spoke to them, saying, "All authority has been given to Me in heaven and on earth" (Matthew 28:18).

All power and authority are given to Him, and therefore creation is to submit to His rulership. As the head, the Spirit of Yeshua is the first from among the dead and is the chief cornerstone. Just as humanity was once in Adam, so now are all who believe in Yeshua in the original place of authority, returned to the will of the Father.

> For through Him we both have our access in one Spirit to the Father. So then you are no longer strangers and aliens, but you are fellow citizens with the saints, and are of God's household, having been built on the foundation of the apostles and prophets, Christ Jesus Himself being the corner stone, in whom the whole building, being fitted together, is growing into a holy temple in the Lord (Ephesians 2:18-20).

## Vav

*Vav* (ו) is the next letter in the word *ruach*. As previously discussed this letter connects in order to continue. It is the spirit of a man that sustains. Yeshua, represented in the letter *vav*, fixes, unites and bonds all that call on His name.

> For there is one God and one mediator also between God and men, the man Yeshua HaMashiach

(Salvation, the Anointed One), who gave Himself as a ransom for all (1 Timothy 2:5).

Yeshua ransomed man in order to transform him into a new creation. Yeshua serves as the tent peg or the nail that has qualified humanity to once again inherit light. We have been rescued from the domain of darkness and transferred into the beloved. Vav is also in the Tetragammaton, YH<u>V</u>H. Notice how vav stands between two of the same letter *hei*. Hei is a breath letter. It is Yeshua as the mediator who connects breath to breath, life to life, and man's spirit back to God. The Ruach quickens in order to bring life. As the Word of God, Yeshua fills in the space where man was unable to connect to God.

> Blessed be the God and Father of our Lord Jesus Christ, who in his great mercy gave us a new birth to a living hope through the resurrection of Jesus Christ from the dead (1 Peter 1:3).

With the numerical value of six this letter begins with a man and ends with the Man. Six represents labor, incompleteness and the weakness of man. Yeshua finishes the work set before Him, bringing liberty from sin. The nails of the cross were set in place so that those who believed would obtain life. Vav stands vertically, signifying the uprightness of Yeshua. In the letter *vav* man comes to God through the rightness of Yeshua.

## Chet

*Chet* (ח) is the final letter in the word *ruach*. It is the eighth Hebrew letter and has a numerical value of eight. The letter *chet*, pronounced "het," represents the transcendence of grace and life. Creation was formed in six days with the seventh day serving as a time of rest; the eighth day became a new beginning. The number eight, therefore, is considered the number of new beginnings.

Adam was made a living soul by the breath of God, which gave Adam his beginning. At the fall of Adam he lost the connection with God and began to live from his soul (his mind, will and emotions). When this occurred, Adam experienced a new beginning involving weakness, hopelessness and deficiencies that limited him as God's representative.

Chet serves as the new beginning whereby mankind is able to transcend human frailty through the grace of God, through His blessing that causes us to be what we were intended to be. The word for God's loving-kindness in Hebrew is *chesed* and is linked to grace. Chesed is unmotivated and unconditional. It is God's ultimate love toward mankind as the image and likeness of God. True kindness is defined as giving something for nothing.

But God, being rich in mercy, because of His great love with which He loved us, even when we were dead in our transgressions, made us alive together with Christ (by grace you have been saved), and raised us up with Him, and seated us with Him in the heavenly places in Christ Jesus, so that in the ages to come He might show the surpassing riches of His grace in kindness toward us in Christ Jesus. For by grace you have been saved through faith; and that not of yourselves, it is the gift of God; not as a result of works, so that no one may boast (Ephesians 2:4-9).

The number eight is also the number for resurrection. Resurrection facilitates a new beginning through the Ruach. Yeshua is the resurrection because, through His life, a new beginning occurs.

Jesus told her, "I am the resurrection and the life; whoever believes in Me, even if he dies, will live, and everyone who lives and believes in Me will never die" (John 11:25-26).

If Christ is in you, though the body is dead because of sin, yet the spirit is alive because of righteousness. But if the Spirit of Him who raised Jesus from the dead dwells in you, He who raised Christ Jesus from the dead will also give life to your mortal bodies through His Spirit who dwells in you (Romans 8:10-11).

Chet is the letter in which worship is restored because of man's ability to live again in the newness of eternal life gained through resurrection. God's kingdom is the rule and reign of His Word. Yeshua is the way, truth and life of worship. In God's kingdom His servants, the sons and daughters, have the responsibility to respond to God in obedience just as Yeshua did while on earth.

Therefore from now on we recognize no one according to the flesh; even though we have known Christ according to the flesh, yet now we know Him in this way no longer. Therefore if anyone is in Christ, he is a new creature; the old things passed away; behold, new things have come. Now all these things are from God, who reconciled us to Himself through Christ and gave us the ministry of reconciliation (2 Corinthians 5:16-18).

The pictograph of the letter *chet* appears as a ladder resting on its side. It is a picture of a tent wall with sections. The function of the wall was to protect the inhabitants of the tent; Yeshua is the hedge that keeps the believer protected. We must live by the Ruach so that we are led in all truth.

If we are children of God, then we are led by the Spirit of God.

Being led by the Spirit and not by one's soul requires a person to walk circumspectly in order to command. Because the walk is submitted under the authority of God, the person then is able to command the actions of the mind, will and emotions. When a person walks according to the mind, will and emotions of the flesh, the circumstances of life will dictate that they find themselves being commanded by some-thing other than the Ruach. There is no compromise. When believers compromise they lose their place of authority. Yeshua has stripped the enemy of all power and given us the place above the enemy.

> For to this you have been called, because Christ also suffered for you, leaving you an example that you should follow in His footsteps. He committed no sin, and no deceit was found in His mouth (1 Peter 2:21-22).

Chet employs God's grace to surpass compromise because the Ruach directs the conduct of the believer. Galatians 5:16 tells us to walk by the Spirit and not to carry out the desires of the flesh. Yeshua is the living example, which clearly gives life empowered by the Ruach.

Chet, as the letter of new beginnings, conveys the mission of repentance. Returning to God has only one purpose: to worship Him in spirit and truth. In Hebraic tradition worship is service, and service is obedience. The greatest example of worship is the way we are to follow the Ruach HaKodesh.

> But an hour is coming, and now is, when the true worshipers will worship the Father in spirit and truth; for such people the Father seeks to be His worshipers.

God is spirit, and those who worship Him must worship in spirit and truth (John 4:23-24).

The Ruach in Judaism is the divine spark of spirit of Adonai which imbues all mankind. The ancient Jewish sages used the word *ruach* as the prescribed spiritual blueprint of man held in Adonai's mind before being breathed into life, or Adam Kadmon (Qadmon)—(Adam before). The word *qadim* is rendered as "east," "ancient" and "that which will come." Keeping in mind there was no "Western world," the original "Eastern spirit" evolved into a Western world movement which would later be called the Holy Spirit within Christianity.

The Ruach or the "Ancient Spirit" to the sages is seen as the spirit of mankind that had been alienated in the world from God until Mashiach. Daniel 7:8-23 records "Attiq Yomin" in Aramaic "Ancient of Days" is the expressed revelation of God as the one who sits upon the throne as divine. Ruach or the Spirit in ancient context is the path which returns God's vision (ability to see His way) as originally designed to mankind.

## Dvar

The most common Hebrew expression for "the Word" in Hebrew is *dvar* sometimes shown as *devar* (דבר), which can mean "word," "thing," "matter" or "affair." Dvar implies content and reality in one's words. It is the viable link between God and His earthly creation. In Aramaic it is the word *memra*. In the Greek language it is *logos*. I want to discuss the words *devar* and *memra* to bring to light the life of God's Word in Yeshua. Devar is comprised of three letters reading from left to right: dalet, bet and reish.

## Dalet

*Dalet* (ד) is the fourth letter and has a numerical value of four. Dalet means "door" and has the shape of an open door. The basic significance of dalet has been discussed already, but I would like to associate dalet with the function of the Ruach. It is critical to remember that all creation is made by the word of God. According to the sages, dalet is seen as that which receives charity from the rich. Charity is a concept of justice in Hebraic thinking; it deals with the relief of unfairness, especially that experienced by orphans, widows and the poor. Charity is blessing through lovingkindness. Dalet, being a door, is the opening that receives as well as gives. It signifies selflessness because it has nothing of its own.

A door is a wonderful illustration of the power of free choice. Yeshua is the dalet to those that choose to enter. Dalet's association to dvar is vital in understanding the Ruach.

> I am the door; if anyone enters through Me, he will be saved, and will go in and out and find pasture (John 10:9).

Yeshua describes the movement of the believer as "through Me" because He is the way. Every believer comes to the Father through the only door by choice. The choice Adam made remains for all who were in Adam. There is divine will, and there is free choice, the will of a person. God gives all the power to fulfill His will. Most believers encounter problems when the flesh steps in; they sometimes begin to believe in their own personal strength and intelligence outside of God. Free will was originally the willingness of man to participate actively in God's will. It is the original intention of will that dalet is connected to God's Word. Yeshua, by the Spirit of God, came into being because of selflessness. The Word emptied itself of divinity to take on the likeness of flesh, thereby becoming the door, which gave and received.

All of Yeshua's essence and being came from God. The Word forms the will of God and brings God's intentions into reality. The Lord's ultimate kindness is His Word. Dalet is the living example of coming in and going out within the Word of God by His Spirit.

## Bet

Bet (ב) is the second letter and has a numerical value of two. It means "house." All of creation is housed in the letter *bet*. Bet is the first letter used in "b'reishit," which means "in the beginning" (בראשית).

Bet is the first letter in b'reishit, since Hebrew is read from right to left. This letter, as "house," is the "interior" letter so to speak. It is that which expresses "within." When looking at a house, the external is not important for living; it is the internal that matters. Though the external may have an appeal, it is the inside that matters to a person when building a home. Bet is that letter that houses all that was going to be created from the beginning. God is this beginning because He is the Creator of all that is made.

All that the Lord has created is from within; therefore it is His heart. The greatest commandment is to love the Lord with all your heart, soul and mind. Love is key to God's sending forth His Word to build a dwelling place for Himself. The Hebrew word for heart is *lev* (לב).

Lev translates as "authority" because it is the center or innermost being of a person that brings action. Out of the abundance of the heart the mouth speaks, according to Matthew 12:34 and Luke 6:45. The letter *bet* in the Hebrew word for heart (*lev*) ends as the same letter that begins the record of creation. Lev ends with the letter *bet* and begins with lamed (study). The summation of heart is in the word *avodah*, which refers to divine service. The highest form of worship is the study of God's Word; from the Hebraic perspective learning is seeking out justice and grace for all.

The connection of bet to this is that it attaches a person to the Lord, who houses all things. All of creation is housed in the Word of God and drawn to reflect who He is by His Ruach.

The final letter in devar is reish. Reish is the twentieth letter and carries a numerical value of two hundred. Reish literally means "there is a beginning." Devar ends with the letter that declares the Word to be the beginning, the head or the chief of all. The Ruach is the Word of God. Reish begins and ends the word for Ruach and devar. Reish, when it comes to the Spirit of God, serves as the beginning of all worship through the Word.

Reish's value of two hundred represents glory, honor and abundance; yet two hundred also represents insufficiency (see Joshua 7:21; 2 Samuel 14:26, 18:9; Judges 17:4, 18; Ezra 2:65).

The Word of God reveals His glory. Glory in Hebrew is *kavod*. The kavod of God is more than sufficient as the beginning of all and is therefore worthy of all. Yeshua glorified is the unbroken, all-sufficient incarnate Word that lives by the Spirit of God. Kavod is rooted in *kavad* alluding to grace within glory which gives us our beginning.

kavod: ד + ו+ ב+ כ/ $4 + 6 + 2 + 20 = (32) = 3 + 2 = 5$
kavad: ד + ב+ כ/ $4 + 2 + 20 = (26) = 2 + 6 = 8$

The word *kavad* has the same numerical value, twenty-six, as the sacred name YHVH. When broken down to its simplest number kavad is reduced to eight, which is the number for resurrection or beginning. The fear of the Lord is the beginning of wisdom and is the foundation to experiencing the glory of God through His grace. The word *glory* in Hebraic context is a palm of a hand bending the willing into submission. The priests were unable to stand when God's glory came because one of the functions of glory is to bend into submission.

Glory is often associated with the Shekinah. Shekinah is from the root word *shekan* meaning "to dwell" or "to lodge." It is a verb; therefore there is action. Shekinah is the dwelling or tangible presence of God. It is the aspect of God which takes up residence and dwells particularly in the tabernacle. There is a distinct difference between the Ruach [Spirit] and Shekinah. According to the ancient rabbis, the distinction was associated with the first temple of Jerusalem and what was missing from the second temple. It is speculated that the Shekinah outwardly emanated from the Holy of Holies of the first temple. Both the shekinah and glory are the same in some ways; yet in function they differ. The shekinah is what takes up active dwelling in a particular place; the glory is the result of this action.

The Word is *memra* in Aramaic. Memra comes from a Hebrew and Aramaic root word which means "to say." Memra corresponds to the Hebrew word *devar*. The memra is a mediator between the unapproachable God and the creature man. The numerical value of memra is 281. [mem (40) + aleph (1) + mem (40) + reish (200) = 281 = 2 + 8 + 1 = 11 = 1 + 1 = 2]

Two is an important number because it symbolically represents witness, testimony and balance. It is also the number of truth and incarnation. Two is the first number that is divisible, and it describes a double-edged sword in Hebrews 4:12. When God's original state is placed in proper perspective, the spirit and soul are separated, as well as the bone and marrow.

Psalm 147:15 describes the Word as running, saying, "He sends forth His command to the earth; His word runs very swiftly." In Isaiah 55:10-11, the Word goes out and accomplishes the will of God.

For as the rain and the snow come down from heaven, and do not return there without watering the earth and making it bear and sprout, and furnishing seed to the sower and bread to the eater; so will My word be which goes forth from My mouth; it will not return to Me empty, without accomplishing what I desire, and without succeeding in the matter for which I sent it. For just as from the heavens the rain and snow come down and do not return there till they have watered the earth, making it fertile and fruitful, giving seed to him who sows and bread to him who eats, so shall My word be that goes forth from My mouth; it shall not return to Me void, but shall do My will, achieving the end for which I sent it.

In the liturgy of the church, which was adopted from the synagogue, it is especially interesting to notice how often the term *logos*, the Greek word for the "memra," in the sense of 'the Word by which God made the world, or made His Law or Himself known to man,' was changed into 'Christ.' Possibly on account of the Christian dogma, rabbinic theology, outside of the Targum literature, made little use of the term *memra*.[5]

When John wrote his Gospel, he was fully aware of the use of the word *memra* as an appearance of God to men; this was common usage during his day. Jewish theologians of John's era ascribed six attributes to the memra. John assigned every attribute to Yeshua in the first chapter of his Gospel. The attributes are:

1. The memra is individual and yet the same as God ("And the Word was with God, and the Word was God," John 1:1).
2. The memra was the instrument of creation ("All things were made by Him," John 1:3, and "the world was made by him," John 1:10).
3. The memra was the instrument of salvation ("But as many as received Him, to them gave He power

to become the sons of God, even to them that believe on His name," John 1:12).

4. The memra was the visible presence of God or Theophany ("And the Word was made flesh and dwelt among us," John 1:14).
5. The memra was the covenant-maker ("For the law was given by Moses, but grace and truth came by Jesus Christ," John 1:17).
6. The memra was the revealer of God ("No man hath seen God at any time; the only begotten Son, which is in the bosom of the Father, he hath declared him," John 1:18 KJV).[6]

The Word of God's sole purpose is to return to man the breath of God, which carried holiness. The Word of God is the transferring of man into the ranks of the redeemed. When the Holy Spirit is active, there is the process of personal wholeness, where personal integrity exists at every level. Man as a living creature lives by drawing in the breath of God. God exhaled into Adam when man became a living soul. True salvation is the fulfillment of God's purpose and design. Sin at the most basic level is not to be the fullness in the image and likeness of God.

Yeshua is the Word accomplished and returned to God. All other names of Yeshua within the armor are there as fortification. The Word is not something that is read from a book, but a living person. Paul ends his description of the armor with the Word because the Word is eternal. It comes from eternity from an eternal God. Yeshua is the eternal Word of God, and this is salvation. It is in the grace of God that all of humanity is restored to the place of God's rule and reign through the Lordship of Yeshua.

Armor is living and breathing, just as Adam is the "speaking" spirit; he was the only created being able to relate to God. Yeshua as the Word fulfilled, having obeyed, is the speaking Spirit of God. I have given six names that show Yeshua's active role of reconciling creation to the Creator as the Word.

Emet—Truth
Ish Tzaddik—Righteous One (Man)
Yehoshua—Salvation
Emunah—Faithful Witness
Sar Shalom—Prince of Peace
Ruach/Devar/Memra—Spirit/Word

The number six is the number of man because man was created on the sixth day (Genesis 1:26-31). Six men testified to the Word prior to Yeshua's crucifixion. The testimony of six establishes the name of Yeshua and God's Word in both heaven and earth.

Pilate—Luke 23:14
Herod—Luke 23:8-12
Judas—Matthew 27:3
Pilate's Wife—Matthew 27:19
The Dying Thief—Luke 23:41
Centurion—Luke 23:47

It is the testimony of man that will declare the glory of God through redemption. Redemption is the regeneration of man's spirit by the Spirit of God. Yeshua is the character and nature of being translated from death to life.

Giving thanks to the Father, who has qualified us to share in the inheritance of the saints in light. For He rescued us from the domain of darkness, and transferred us to the kingdom of His beloved Son, in whom we have redemption, the forgiveness of sins. He is the image of the invisible God, the firstborn of all creation. For by Him all things were created, both in the heavens and on earth, visible and invisible, whether thrones or dominions or rulers or authorities—all things have been created through Him and for Him. He is before all things, and in Him all things hold together. He is also head of the body, the church; and He is the beginning, the firstborn from the dead, so that He Himself will come to have first place in everything. For it was the Father's good pleasure for all the fullness to dwell in Him (Colossians 1:12-19).

The armor has a metaphoric meaning as well as a deeper insight into the person of Yeshua. Salvation is the covering to them that believe and receive Yeshua. As the head of the body, Yeshua is the covering for the spirit, soul and body. When Adam left the garden, the soul needed a covering; this is what flesh is all about. Sin is the covering that resulted in the awareness of self. The revelation of salvation (Yeshua) is the redemptive covering which restores mankind's spirit. Every name demonstrated in the armor has an authority that cannot be violated because of the obedience of Yeshua. The Word returned to the place it came from, fulfilled and accomplished, with no void.

In Christian theology and the canonization of the Bible for the Greek mindset, Paul refers to Yeshua as the "last Adam." Yeshua is not the last Adam as presented but is the last word in relation to God's image and likeness. When Yeshua says, "It is finished," He is declaring there is nothing more to say because He is the "I AM," the final word; there is nothing more. Paul encourages the believers to be strong in the "I AM" and to stand.

Man was once spiritually aware of his Creator, but by the disobedience of man sinful flesh covered that awareness. Yeshua is this correction, as the restoration and reconciliation. By destroying the law of sin which held us captive to the flesh, Yeshua in fullness is now the revelation of God and thereby returns man to communion with God. Yeshua is the living armor for the spiritual man that covers every person who believes in Him. It is the character and nature that now separate us once again from the Lord.

We must go all the way back to what takes place in the garden in Genesis 1–3 to regain the understanding of who we are in God through the work of Yeshua. In capturing the original intention of God we must embrace the fullness of Yeshua as the Word in the person of image and likeness. Every believer in Yeshua is to reflect back to God, not in earthly nature but in the redeemed nature because of the new covering of Yeshua. In this new place it is in heaven as it is on earth, and what now covers us is salvation; the battle is really the Lord's.

## To the Rear
The armor of the Lord implies those things that cover the front of the person. Though Roman armor did cover a soldier's back, Paul does not include the rear as an essential part of his discourse. One would think a person's back in warfare would be crucial since most successful military strategy involves approaching an enemy from the rear. Wars in the natural occur for various reasons—mainly the desire for sovereign independence or some valuable territorial land. Though physical war is brutal, violent and devastating, warfare is not physical for believers. The covering provided in the Lord's armor differs in relation to natural warfare.

> Finally, be strong in the Lord and in the strength of His might. Put on the full armor of God, so that you will be able to stand firm against the schemes of the devil. For our struggle is not against flesh and blood, but against the rulers, against the powers,

against the world forces of this darkness, against the spiritual forces of wickedness in the heavenly places (Ephesians 6:1-3).

What was the original scheme of Satan prior to the veil of flesh? Flesh as we know it today was not in place; therefore the byproduct of the sin nature—that is, lust-of-the-flesh, lust-of-the-eyes and pride-of-life issues—is not the issue for Satan. Sin was not yet a seed in Adam in the original state of his makeup. Satan was after something greater, resulting in what many struggle with. It was the attack on Adam's identity as the image and likeness of God.

To get the picture of what covers the back I must explain eternity and how time relates to it within the context of God's intention. To the ancient Hebrews eternity, or the Hebrew word *olam,* was not "never ending." Olam is a pictorial concept more than it is a specific word definition. Olam gives the picture of a horizon where one looks out across land or water and sees the sun touching the earth. As nomadic people, the Hebrews would look out seeing this picture and call it olam. It could imply eternity. This is because the place where the sun appeared to touch the earth is as far as the natural eye could see, but they understood more was still beyond that point. They knew their eyes could see only so far from the position of looking out; this was eternity—what was on the other side of the sun. Olam is the place where light gathers.

The second concept to picture is time in relation to the past and the future. The past was seen as something in front of a person, and the future was behind. This perception of time is totally opposite to today's thinking. For the ancient Hebrews the past is in front of a person because it can be seen, and the future is behind because it cannot be seen. With this in mind the future being behind as the unseen is where Adam originated. The natural mind cannot perceive that place. It is beyond our ability to see from this realm because of the veil of flesh. The future is the place where light (revelation) gathers in God, our original perception. Remember that light is not seen but makes seeing possible. The first thing God created was light so that revelation could manifest creation. Adam travelled with God by perception, and this was at the speed of light, so to speak.

We had a glory or substance in God that enabled us to be the image and likeness of God, something Satan despised. Satan was not interested in creation but the crown of creation which was mankind. This crown would have given him a false sense of "lordship," his desire from the time of his demise.

With the future behind you then would it not make sense that redemption in Yeshua covers our rear? There is no need for armor at the rear when victory is already in place as believers look toward the unseen eternal things. Restoration of mankind as a future event is actually behind us, not in front of us. God really does have your back or better said our future. Yeshua has returned us to glorious kingdom authority. Our future is in the restoration of who we are in God through salvation.

> Yours, O Lord, is the greatness and the power and the glory and the victory and the majesty, indeed everything that is in the heavens and the earth; Yours is the dominion, O Lord, and You exalt Yourself as head over all (1 Chronicles 29:11-12).

> Violence will not be heard again in your land, nor devastation or destruction within your borders; but you will call your walls salvation, and your gates praise. No longer will you have the sun for light by day, nor for brightness will the moon give you light; but you will have the Lord for an everlasting light, and your God for your glory. Your sun will no longer

set, nor will your moon wane; for you will have the Lord for an everlasting light, and the days of your mourning will be over (Isaiah 60:18-20).

Throughout the recorded Gospels the Jewish disciples who believed Yeshua as Mashiach came to look beyond the Roman oppression which served as their enemy. The attacks Israel had endured over the centuries had left the nation in a state of hopelessness and despair; yet with the arrival of Yeshua the disciples saw a greater light and received a better revelation as to who they were as covenanted people. In 2 Corinthians 4, Paul gives a wonderful discourse of an earthen treasure and how the unseen things are eternal. Today as people of covenant, whether as a Jewish or Gentile believer, the armor conveys that the future in Yeshua is beyond the current realm of sight. What covers our rear is in the things to come, a place of timelessness where all things perceived are eternal.

For God so loved the world, that He gave His only begotten Son, that whoever believes in Him shall not perish, but have eternal life (John 3:16).

# Chapter Twelve:

# Prayer, the Final Frontier

"With all prayer and petition pray at all times in the Spirit, and with this in view, be on the alert with all perseverance and petition for all the saints" (Ephesians 6:18).

**P**aul ends his armor discourse with prayer. Prayer in Hebrew is *tefillah*. Paul followed the traditions of Jewish prayers. Standing began his message because standing is important in prayer according to the Jewish way of life. Though we stand during prayer, the heart is humbly submitted to God. When we stand fully redeemed with no condemnation, the full authority of heaven will manifest itself. Tefillah means "to judge oneself." Prayer is an integral part of everyday life for the observant Jew.

But thou, when thou prayest, enter into thy closet, and when thou hast shut thy door, pray to thy Father which is in secret; and thy Father which seeth in secret shall reward thee openly. But when ye pray, use not vain repetitions, as the heathen do: for they think that they shall be heard for their much speaking. Be not ye therefore like unto them: for your Father knoweth what things ye have need of, before ye ask him (Matthew 6:6-8 KJV).

Prayer is done through something known as *kavanah*, which is being intentional through concentration. Paul was encouraging the people to remain intentional in all things concerning Yeshua. There are several aspects of kavanah. The first is that a person must know what he is saying, and the second is that a person must know to whom he is speaking. It is believed among the rabbis when a person prays and doesn't know to whom he is praying, there is no prayer. Tefillah means to stand and converse with God. If the mind wanders during prayer, likewise, there is no prayer.

Paul valued the concept of prayers entering into a realm beyond the physical. As a new creation in Yeshua, one finds a new form of worshipping God in spirit and in truth. Tefillah is outward at the same time that it is actively inward. It is not the words said that are important, but the intention. Prayer is the realm where change occurs. Prayer is to be done intentionally in order to gain the intention of God, not His attention. God is very much aware of all creation. He seeks to bring His purposes day to day through our faithfulness.

Paul tells the people to stay in Yeshua and seek the Father's will. Yeshua taught this to His disciples through the model of the Amidah. The Amidah was central to Jewish life during the time of Yeshua as it still is today. During the biblical period prayer in a Hebraic sense was considered a commandment and an appointed time.

Prayer is considered a commandment according to Deuteronomy 11:13, where it reads, "It shall come about, if you listen obediently to My commandments which I am commanding you today, to love the Lord your God and to serve Him with all your heart and all your soul." To serve the Lord was an act of the heart. The place of serving God was in the heart during prayer; this service is referred to as "Avodah sheba-Lev" (service from the heart).

The appointed times of prayer were according to the traditions of the patriarchs and temple sacrifice times. Sages believed Abraham represented the morning prayer, Isaac represented the afternoon prayer, and Jacob represented the final time during the evening prayer.

> You shall fear the Lord your God; you shall serve Him and cling to Him, and you shall swear by His name (Deuteronomy 10:20).

Prayer within a Christian setting is to draw closer to God, but it is not to cling to Him necessarily. It is mainly about request, worship and then walking away until the next time. In the Bible prayer is both for an appointed time and spontaneous when giving thanks.

Rabbinic writings document prayers being offered in various districts throughout Israel at the times of the temple sacrifices. The timing of prayer is very important. There must be an appointed time for prayer to have a place. This is foreign to most Christians, who see prayer as an activity outside of work.

> Now when Daniel knew that the document was signed, he entered his house; now in his roof chamber he had windows open toward Jerusalem; and he continued kneeling on his knees three times a day, praying and giving thanks before his God, as he had been doing previously (Daniel 6:10).

Daniel refers to an appointed time at which prayer and sacrifices were offered. He is known to have prayed at certain times while setting his face toward Jerusalem. In exile Daniel could not offer the appointed sacrifices at the temple, so a time of prayer became his daily sacrifices.

During the biblical time Israel was divided into twenty-four districts or precincts. These districts were on rotation to serve as eyewitnesses to the daily sacrifices at the temple in Jerusalem. These eyewitnesses were known as the "standing men of the station" or "men of prayer." To insure the witness of each tribe, a temple tax was paid by all Israel to provide for the morning and afternoon sacrifices; in essence, everyone gave toward the sacrifice. In the temple at this time the men offered praise and prayer while the sacrifice was performed, and at the same time other men would pray in their district (see Exodus 29:38-46).

During the morning sacrifice the Shachrit prayers (from *shachar,* "morning light") were recited. During the afternoon sacrifice the Mincha prayers (from the flour/grain offering associated with sacrifice) were recited. The final prayers were Ma'ariv/Arvit (from nightfall) for the evening. This prayer was connected to the burning of the sacrificial leftovers.

In the New Testament prayer is fundamental to worship for the first believers in Yeshua. There is biblical evidence of how the first believers prayed during specific times of the day. The custom of praying at times of sacrifices was observed by Yeshua as well as other Jews.

> When the day of Pentecost had come, they were all together in one place. And suddenly there came from heaven a noise like a violent rushing wind, and it filled the whole house where they were sitting. And there appeared to them tongues as of fire distributing themselves, and they rested on each one of them. And they were all filled with the Holy Spirit and began to speak with other tongues, as the Spirit was giving them utterance. . . . But Peter, taking his stand with the eleven, raised his voice and declared to them:

"Men of Judea and all you who live in Jerusalem, let this be known to you and give heed to my words. For these men are not drunk, as you suppose, for it is only the third hour of the day" (Acts 2:1-4, 14-15).

This third hour was nine o'clock in the morning, a time of sacrifice. Mark 15:24-25 says, "And they crucified Him, and divided up His garments among themselves; casting lots for them to decide what each man should take. It was the third hour when they crucified Him." Later in the same chapter of Mark, verses 33-39 read,

> When the sixth hour came, darkness fell over the whole land until the ninth hour. At the ninth hour Jesus cried out with a loud voice, "ELOI, ELOI, LAMA SABACHTHANI?" which is translated, "MY GOD, MY GOD, WHY HAVE YOU FORSAKEN ME?" When some of the bystanders heard it, they began saying, "Behold, He is calling for Elijah." Someone ran and filled a sponge with sour wine, put it on a reed, and gave Him a drink, saying, "Let us see whether Elijah will come to take Him down." And Jesus uttered a loud cry, and breathed His last. And the veil of the temple was torn in two from top to bottom. When the centurion, who was standing right in front of Him, saw the way He breathed His last, he said, "Truly this man was the Son of God."

The sixth hour is around noon, and the ninth hour is approximately three o'clock in the afternoon. The first believers were gathered during the ninth hour of the day at the time of the sacrifice. Yeshua is the sacrifice in Mark.

Prayer was part of the entire worship process among Jews and the first believers who were Jews. Acts 2:42 says,

"They were continually devoting themselves to the apostles' teaching and to fellowship, to the breaking of bread and to prayer."

This following passage occurred during afternoon prayer at the second sacrifice:

> A devout man and one who feared God with his entire household, and gave much alms to the Jewish people and prayed to God continually. About the ninth hour of the day he clearly saw in a vision an angel of God who had just come in and said to him, "Cornelius!" (Acts 10:2-3).

The temple was for offering sacrifices and for prayer. These passages relate to prayer at appointed times. Typically the temple was not a place of fellowship or just "hanging out." In the temple there was always a purpose within the customs of the day. Most hardworking citizens didn't have time for fellowship under Roman rule. Fellowship and edifying took place in homes.

> When the governor had nodded for him to speak, Paul responded: "Knowing that for many years you have been a judge to this nation, I cheerfully make my defense, since you can take note of the fact that no more than twelve days ago I went up to Jerusalem to worship" (Acts 24:10-11).

The idea behind praying with kavanah is that the direction of thinking is set completely toward God. Prayer is a reaching in to reach out. It is looking inside and seeing a person's role within creation in their relationship with God.

Paul wanted to stress the importance of unity through prayer. As a Hebrew, Paul's greatest concern was maintaining unity as the body, as Israel had done for centuries. He knew that without unity the door to idolatry and immorality would open. When the first believers gathered, unity was the principal point. Just as they stood as one nation on Mount Sinai, Israel was to be the light to the world, with the sole purpose of repairing the breach between God and man. For Jewish believers in Yeshua the kingdom of God of the first century was established on three pillars.

1. To encounter Yeshua
2. The role of Torah
3. Prayer

Paul was very much aware of these three pillars. The kingdom of God, as seen in the book of Acts, was very much the dominion of Yeshua in the unity of His name as the kingdom of God increased through those who believed. In his conclusion Paul is continuing in the awareness of God's presence at all times. Yeshua has ascended into the hill of the Lord and is the mediator for God's will. Salvation is the covering whereby every believer is able to stand, having overcome darkness and deception. Yeshua said the pure in heart are blessed, for they see God (see Matthew 5:8). As joint heir in and with Mashiach, we as sons and daughters of the El Elyon (Most High God) can ascend into the Lord (see Romans 8:16-18).

Who may ascend into the hill of the Lord? And who may stand in His holy place? He who has clean hands and a pure heart (Psalm 24:3).

# Conclusion:

# Original Identity

Then I heard a loud voice saying in heaven, "Now salvation, and strength, and the kingdom of our God, and the power of His Christ have come, for the accuser of our brethren, who accused them before our God day and night, has been cast down" (Revelation 12:10).

B eing born again is the restoration of dominion and authority as originally intended by God when man was first made. Life in the beginning was not in the flesh as we comprehend it to be today; therefore our identity cannot be achieved nor perceived in the flesh. Identity is something inherited as part of who we are.

Life in the flesh consists of the genetic makeup known as DNA, or deoxyribonucleic acid. To the spiritually minded, science may not immediately come to mind. Unfortunately science can seem incompatible with a spiritual God; yet to ignore science is a mistake. Everything was created by the Creator; there is nothing in creation that did not come from Him.

DNA is found in genes, in chromosomes, in the nucleus of a cell. In short, DNA is a nucleic acid that carries the genetic information in the cell and is capable of self-replication and synthesis of RNA. DNA consists of two long chains of nucleotides twisted into a double helix and joined by hydrogen bonds between the complementary bases adenine and thymine or cytosine and guanine. The sequence of nucleotides determines individual hereditary characteristics.[7]

> For the life of the flesh is in the blood, and I have given it to you on the altar to make atonement for your souls; for it is the blood by reason of the life that makes atonement (Leviticus 17:11).

Who we are is more than flesh and blood; the life of every creature, however, is in the blood. The very essence of the Creator is in the blood because it was in the blood that God placed His existence that now gives us life. Blood is critical to maintaining human life because the blood carries the intention of God's plan in man. Blood is the substance that carries oxygen, or the Ruach of God, to every part of the body. When oxygen fails to reach a certain part of the body, death occurs.

Why is understanding DNA important for believers and the armor of the Lord? The answer is in knowing that DNA is historical memory in the flesh realm. Both the visible and invisible characteristics of our ancestors are in the genetic makeup of who we are. DNA carries the history of what we have done in the human body. Our parents can pass on hereditary diseases, personalities, curses due to rebellion or unconfessed sins. DNA is the written code within every person at the level of flesh.

The genetic makeup of the spirit is the Word of God. The armor of the Lord is not something to be put on daily. The armor is the DNA (divine nature authority) whereby believers step into, to walk as. Paul admonishes to stand, having done all; it is Yeshua who has done all, and therefore it is His battle as Lord. Every believer overcomes by the blood of the Lamb and the word of personal testimony. What is personal about a testimony is the power of the author; this is authority. Yeshua is the author and finisher of faithfulness because Adam failed at showing himself faithful. Mankind lost his authority when God's Word ceased being the rule. At one point we were not "mankind" but "man-king" of God's creation, able to rule according to the Master's will.

God's Word is eternal and serves as the "divine nature authority" of God in the spiritual makeup of man. In John 20:22 Yeshua breathes and tells the disciples to receive the *pneuma hagion* (Holy Spirit). John 20:22 in the Greek translation conveys a fixed position as in time, space or state in order to beget.[8] Grammatically speaking it is in the same tense and person as used in the Septuagint (ancient Greek translation of the Pentateuch) in Genesis 2:7. There is a correlation between Yeshua blowing the Ruach HaKodesh into the disciples in John 20:22 and God blowing the breath of life into Adam in Genesis 2:7.

The armor of the Lord is not only the covering by which we experience the character and nature of Yeshua through the reputation (name), but it is also the DNA where the "divine nature of authority" is the code that reestablishes true identity. When people humble themselves they once again see as God does. In Genesis 3, Satan introduced the ego, the self, saying that man would be like God, knowing good and evil. But instead of seeing more man saw less or at best saw only fifty percent of creation because of flesh, and seeing became what is visible to the natural eyes.

The invisible realm was "seen" prior to Adam's eyes being opened. The warfare experienced by believers is spiritual because believers are spiritual beings, the true self.

Now those who belong to Christ Jesus have crucified the flesh with its passions and desires. If we live by the Spirit, let us also walk by the Spirit (Galatians 5:24-25).

The invisible was not invisible to Adam prior to his disobedience. Mankind lost true sight and insight as the result of Adam's action. When I speak of invisibility I am not referring to how we define the word *invisible*. The invisible is what is covered up. Satan's objective was not to cause man to sin; this would have been a mute point seeing that Adam was not aware of himself in the flesh. Adam was told he would die; better understood, a veil would separate Adam from God. Flesh (covering) separated Adam from God as well as the true spiritual authority and identity Adam walked as. Humanity has been veiled, unable to comprehend the invisible, but Adam and Eve once had the ability to see what is now invisible, or "covered," to us.

The armor of the Lord transmits a much deeper and broader sense in warfare because of the challenges of who we are spiritually. The battle is not in the flesh, though the attacks affect the natural realm. Everything within a person walking in Yeshua is to uphold His name, especially in spiritual warfare. Name is about reputation, authority and character. Names carry great power because it is the nature by purpose. Everything we do is in the name of Yeshua. Everything bows at the name of Yeshua. Yeshua is an active salvation through His obedience and faithfulness. The process of salvation is the placement into one Lord, one Spirit, one faithfulness and one immersion.

There is one body and one Spirit, just as also you were called in one hope of your calling; one Lord, one faith, one baptism, one God and Father of all who is over all and through all and in all (Ephesians 4:4-6).

The reputation of Yeshua is known in both visible and invisible kingdoms. He has gone before and placed dominion back in righteous order. The destiny of every soul is to return to the place from which it came, the place of fruitfulness, multiplicity and dominion where all is subdued. This is what repentance is all about, returning to what is intended for us in God. Everything whether seen or unseen was created to operate according to its nature under the stewardship of man.

For this reason also, God highly exalted Him, and bestowed on Him the name which is above every name, so that at the name of Jesus EVERY KNEE WILL BOW, of those who are in heaven and on earth and under the earth, and that every tongue will confess that Jesus Christ is Lord, to the glory of God the Father (Philippians 2:9-11).

Yeshua (salvation) is the character whereby creation bows. God pointed out two trees in the garden; Adam just chose from the wrong tree. The Etz Chayim (Tree of Life) was available to him and remains to this day; that has never changed. What most Christians do is try to walk with God using the same operating system of knowledge of good and evil. No matter how hard one may try, knowledge is not the platform where we encounter God; we were to never take from it. As sons and daughters we are children that must live in obedience to the Father just as the greatest example did, Yeshua.

Identity is crucial to the kingdom of God, and even more so for those that claim citizenship to it. We are spiritual beings whose exclusivity is in how we live before the Father and the world around us. Mainstream media would have us believe that what we wear, where we live, who we know, how educated we are or how much money a person may or may not have determines our being, but this is furthest from the truth. The kingdom of God is about reigning in a place already accomplished through the King.

Believers of salvation are those who are whole and complete in spirit and soul. They are able to know truth as the substance of God's purpose, a purpose that is the inheritance of power and authority in original dominion. The kingdom of God is the heritage for the born again. The realm of this heritage is God's rule and reign in the realm of blessing. The kingdom of God is the restorative identity in Yeshua. This identity is the authority released within the believer to walk as God's agent displacing principalities, changing atmospheres and creating the climate where God can dwell among His creation and people. The revelation of Yeshua is not meant primarily to bring knowledge of who He is, but it is meant to bring relationship back to the Father.

As regenerated beings returned to the Creator of all things, believers are to live as one with the Father just as Yeshua was one with His Father. When the outside world looks into God's kingdom they should see us as different. We walk in the righteous authority. We are to live as truth so that the generations to come will know the Maker of heaven and earth. Our faithfulness is crucial to the faithfulness of the Most High. We are able to go anywhere without hesitation when peace takes us there. As reconciled we carry wholeness. Humanity has been restored to where it all began. The structure of our being can be seen in the six pieces of armor as each piece carries the function by the name of the Lord. It is who we are and not what we do. The armor of the Lord is not something to put on; this could imply the ability to take it off. In regeneration there is nothing more to put on; everything is in place in the restoration.

Every person is called the image and likeness of God and has His nature in salvation. Every believer in Yeshua, as the glory to the Father, is the expression of the Spirit of God. The armor of the Lord is alive with the breath of God. It is appointed by the Lord Himself that we bear His name. Everything within the framework of God is meant to uphold His kingdom through the name above all names. The directive of God's kingdom is to rule and reign.

Satan once challenged man's place by attacking man's identity. During the time of Yeshua in the wilderness with Satan, as Luke 4:13 indicates, Satan left Yeshua for a more opportune time. We never see when this opportune time occurs again in Scripture. I think it is interesting that after John immersed Yeshua, Satan came in to tempt Yeshua. Believers encounter the same pattern of how temptation seems to come after their immersion into the body of Yeshua. Prior to that moment of salvation, we are just serving our flesh; once Yeshua is received Satan looks for a more opportune time within the believer. Satan's mission is to challenge the confession of Yeshua in the believer. He is not tempting the "sinner" anymore but is looking for the opportune time through the believer in Yeshua. Though God Himself cannot be tempted; Satan will tempt God's representative in order to validate or negate the testimony of Yeshua. As the body of Yeshua, believers are the opportune time. Today Satan continues the assault against the body of Yeshua through the believers. Yeshua sums up the only recourse of victory in overcoming the enemy of God in His final response to temptation in Matthew 4:10. Yeshua says, "You shall worship the Lord your God, and serve Him only."

Kingdom identity is the armor where believers must find themselves as and in. The witness of Yeshua's Lordship and kingship is in those that bear His name. It is to uphold with everything within with all our might. God is seeking not what believers do but who He is by the way life is lived day to day. From faithfulness to faithfulness is the only direction believers are to follow in the Spirit, by the spirit. Obedience is the only doctrine that can determine how true our identity is to God, others and ourselves. From the beginning the enemy has repeated the same act of separation by implying believers are not who they are. To seek validation or affirmation of self from anything that is not from the Spirit of God hinders His desire to enlarge Himself within a person. Yeshua is never seen as trying to convince people of who He was to validate His life, ministry or purpose for coming to earth. He walked as commanded and commanded as He walked.

> Now when He was in Jerusalem at the Passover, during the feast, many believed in His name, observing His signs which He was doing. But Jesus, on His part, was not entrusting Himself to them, for He knew all men, and because He did not need anyone to testify concerning man, for He Himself knew what was in man (John 2:23-25).

The function of salvation is wholeness. Yeshua knew who He was and what He was sent to do from the Father. Wholeness includes redemption, restoration, restitution and the reputation of the only One able to achieve this. Yeshua identified with His heavenly Father to the point of oneness. Oneness sounds like something from the new age movement, but this has been the perversion and the deception of the enemy.

The foundation of Judaism is the Shema taken from Deuteronomy 6:4. Echad is one. It denotes to give witness and, in the case of the Shema, the witness to the one Lord who is our God. Israel lived and continues to live this. Yeshua is the "echad" example of God.

Hear, O Israel! The Lord is our God, the Lord is one!

Shma Yisra'el Adonay Eloheynu Adonay Echad.

שמע ישראל יהוה אלהיגו יהוה אחד

Yeshua quotes this as part of His answer to the greatest commandment question (see Mark 12:28-30). It is so important to recognize the value of beginning to embrace the here and now. To serve God with all one's heart, soul, mind and strength requires unity with and in God. Unity is the sameness of commitment and compassion. The Shema is said by most observant Jews at least twice daily. We believe that if we intentionally start and end the day like this then we experience God's kingdom and providence over us.

In the Shema there is hidden a command in the words *shema* (hear/obey) and *echad* (one). The last letters in both words *ayin* in shema and *dalet* in echad when combined allude to the word for witness. Isaiah proclaims, "Etem edai" ("you are my witnesses"), testifying to the unity of Israel's faithful to God.

> "You are My witnesses," declares the Lord, "and My servant whom I have chosen, so that you may know and believe Me and understand that I am He. Before Me there was no God formed, and there will be none after Me" (Isaiah 43:10).

Yeshua was and is the walking witness of wholeness, and as His body believers are to continue in this wholeness. Everything physical has a spiritual purpose which God oversees. Yeshua is recorded as having made this known. He knew nothing could be done without the Father and all could be done with the Father. It is vital that believers are willing to invest their entire selves in the relationship with the Father.

Yeshua is the greatest instance of this. We have a mature example of responsibility and ability through the Word and Spirit of God. Integrity is absolutely necessary and is more important than any spiritual authority when it comes to the uniqueness of unity with the Creator of heaven and earth.

> Then the disciples came to Jesus privately and said, "Why could we not drive it out?" And He said to them, "Because of the littleness of your faith; for truly I say to you, if you have faith the size of a mustard seed, you will say to this mountain, 'Move from here to there,' and it will move; and nothing will be impossible to you" (Matthew 17:19-20).

This passage has been studied, discussed, debated and taught mainly with the focus on the size of the mustard seed. Though this is good theology it does not convey what mattered the most to Yeshua. The mustard seed was important because of the natural makeup of the seed. The mustard seed maintains integrity as a mustard seed. By the nature of the mustard seed it cannot be germinated as any seed other than a mustard seed. Yeshua is concerned with the uprightness of the disciples. What were the character, agendas and motives of their hearts while serving with Yeshua?

In Judaic belief there is no theology of sin, but there is the theology of separation. Adam lost the most precious insight: his identity. The sameness was gone. The oneness with the Father became divided. Searching of self for self including the pleasing of selfish men became our image which became our idol.

Believers today are to have the same mind of the Anointed One in His anointing. Identity is beyond being a "Christian" who goes to church and is active in some "ministerial" capacity. The armor gives us a place to live and be in as we come into unanimity with the names of each part.

Identity is generally defined as the sameness of two things. It is the theory of what is identical, be it theoretical or theological. We have social identity, national identity, class identity, racial and cultural identity, sexual and gender identity, and for the sake of the thieves even digital identity. Though we have many instances by which we can relate to identity they all lack substance when it comes to the core essence of who we are.

"Who am I?" is a common dilemma among the "saved" and "unsaved." Salvation, or "being saved," is not an arrival point when it comes to who we "now" are since we are no longer going to hell. Salvation is the place of departure and return, the departure of question and the return to the answer. Believers are not "saved" so to speak, but they are expected to be "faithful" in covenant through Yeshua.

Not a thing in this world can define the divine in us as sons and daughters. All there is in attempting to characterize ourselves is nothing more than knowledge which leads to death. It is harder to keep up with the "Joneses" than it is just to be who we were designed to be. It is easier to be who God designed us to be rather than what people expect us to be. More than likely the expectations of other people will change like the wind, therefore making it impossible to breathe. It is time for believers to get off the artificial life support and live in the truth of life. I encourage you to take a deep breath of heaven's oxygen. It's cleaner and better for you.

Humanity, regardless of culture, custom, belief and ethnicity, is made in the image and likeness of God. God's kingdom is more than meat and drink. God's kingdom has a divine and eternal destiny. The global communities of believers are truly the envy of Satan and all world systems that oppose God. Though the entire world carries the image and likeness of God by the nature of humanity, those who receive the fullness of God's revelation are able to bless His name with resolute and rest.

The believer's identity is in the name of Yeshua. We have been empowered, endowed and resurrected against all demonic insurrection. We have been restored and renewed to revelation power with the ability to see as God sees. We have divine power, the ability to do what God so desires. We have once again our true voice, the ability to speak as commanded by the Spirit of God. Everything we are to desire is in God because He is to be everything we desire. Kingdom armor is the identity that serves in the name of Yeshua.

People need not acknowledge me with spiritual authority or as someone who has accomplished success through education, financial gain or social status; this is irrelevant for me. I do not seek affirmation to assert myself by nor negation to deny myself as. To live in this yoke is draining because it always demands attention and some audience to applaud it. I along with every other person as a son or daughter must remain within the perimeters of God's kingdom not men's. Adam's failure to remain faithful stripped him of his authority as God's servant. Think about it. If we don't know who we are, then how can we successfully know to be the same in image and likeness as the One who made us?

The error made by most who do know this is their arrogance and pride. Humility is a requirement to God's revelation. Humility is best defined as where the natural ends and the supernatural begins. Pride came before the fall of Satan and the separation of man from God and remains the scales that blind many today. Kingdom identity as it relates to the armor is a covering that uncovers the truth to who we are in unity and totality with the Father.

I remember a time when I was studying the kenosis passage of Philippians 2:7-9. I was doing a word study on *humbled* and found a connection to the word *condescending*. I was puzzled and thought this didn't make sense. I grappled with this for months until the Lord helped me out in a quiet whisper. He said, "I'm God. Do you think there is someone greater than Me? There was no other place for Me to go but down; it was condescending for Me." I then felt myself immediately turn into that heel you see in the cartoons and thought, *Duh?* But then in His infinite love for me I heard Him say, "Therefore that means there is no other place for you to go except up. Sin is the lowest place on earth, son. Come up."After that moment it all fell into place for me as to who I was and where I was in God's kingdom.

To be fearfully and wonderfully made as the expression of the Almighty is such an honor. To be able to serve Him in spirit and truth is liberating as well as God's expectation. Believers are to move past the demarcated lines and outside the boxes while maintaining our godly identity of truth and righteousness, integrity and honor, love and compassion. The world is just a veil, and as part of God's kingdom we are able to be windows into what is beyond that veil. As servants we are responsible to tend not toil as stewards of God. With everything given to us we are to give it completely back to the Father of us all.

Serving in the kingdom of heaven can be perceived in Psalm 103:1: "Bless the Lord, O my soul, and all that is within me, bless His holy name." To appreciate what the passage really conveys as it relates to having kingdom identity, however, it must be viewed in the original context prior to canonization, because to live is His name.

Bless the Lord, O my soul, and all that is within me, HIS HOLY NAME.

**BARUCH HASHEM**
**BLESS THE NAME**

# Endnotes

1.  Etymology: Middle French *identité*, from Late Latin *identitat*, *identitas*, probably from Latin *identidem* repeatedly, contraction of *idem et idem*, literally, "same and same." Date: 1570. http://www. m-w.com/dictionary/identity, 2008.
2.  Rabbi Nosson Scherman, The Chumash, Artscroll Mesorah (Brooklyn, NY: Mesorah Publications, Ltd., 1998), p. 3.
3.  Jeff A. Benner, *A Mechanical Translation of the Book of Genesis* (College Station, TX: VBW Publishing, 2007), p. 21.
4.  Michael Price, *Your Days Are Numbered* (Austin, TX: I AM Publishing, 2003).
5.  *The Jewish Encyclopedia* (New York and London: Littmann, 1904), p. 465.
6.  Carl J. Stevens, *John, the Pharisees, and Memra* © 2000. http:// www.bibleword.org/memra.shtml.
7.  *American Heritage® Dictionary of the English Language* http:// education.yahoo.com/reference/dictionary/entry/DNA.
8.  Key Word Study Bible (KJV) [Concise New Testament; James Strong; Greek Lexicon, pp. 28, 77] (Chattanooga, TN: AMG Publishers, 1984, 1991).

# Bibliography

All references to the ancient Hebrew pictograph are from the *Ancient Hebrew Lexicon of the Bible*, Jeff A. Benner (College Station, TX: VBW Publishing, 2005).

All references to the Hebrew letters and their meanings are from Rabbi Michael L. Munk, *The Wisdom of the Hebrew Alphabet* (Brooklyn, NY: Mesorah Publications, 1983).

All references to numbers and their meaning are from Michael Price, *Your Days Are Numbered* (Austin, TX: International Anointed Ministries, 2003).

To order teachings or for further information,
please contact:

HaMishkan
Rabbi Yisrael ben Avraham
www.tzedakahnow.org
contact@tzedakahnow.org

Printed in the United States
131169LV00001B/169/P

9 781606 476918